STEP OUT-SIDE

STEP OUT~ SIDE

Community~Based Art Education

PETER LONDON

Foreword by David W. Baker

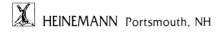
HEINEMANN Portsmouth, NH

For Charles Beck
artist, teacher, friend

HEINEMANN

A division of Reed Publishing (USA) Inc.
361 Hanover Street Portsmouth, NH 03801–3912
Offices and agents throughout the world

Acquisitions editor: Toby Gordon
Production editor: Alan Huisman
Book and cover design: Jenny Jensen Greenleaf
Cover photograph: Ann Schauman, of a public mural in Rochester, New York,
    painted by Jorge Sonarribam with the assistance of Peter Jemison

We would like to thank the children, parents, and teachers who have given their
permission to include material in this book. Every effort has been made to contact
the copyright holders for permission to reprint borrowed material where necessary.
We regret any oversights that may have occurred and would be happy to rectify
them in future printings of this work.

Library of Congress Cataloging-in-Publication Data
London, Peter.
    Step outside : community-based art education / Peter London.
        p.   cm.
    Includes bibliographical references.
    ISBN 0–435-08794-0
    1. Community art projects—United States. 2. Arts—Study and teaching (Ele-
mentary)—United States. 3. Arts—Study and teaching (Secondary)—United
States. I. Title.
NX303.L66 1994
700'.7'073—dc20

                                                        93–11569
                                                        CIP

Printed in the United States of America on acid-free paper
98 97 96 95 94 HP 1 2 3 4 5 6 7 8 9 10

Contents

Foreword

This book's compelling message recognizes the impact communities have on all who grow and develop within them. It further recognizes the vital role community-based instruction in the visual arts can play in promoting and extending learning. It is a message that has great relevance for teachers at all levels of instruction, one that can have a profound impact on curricular practices in all subject areas. In provocative prose and with rich illustration, the author directs one's attention to the essential task of teachers everywhere—to nourish students in ways that enable them to meet their individual needs in a productive manner and, while doing so, to enhance their capacity to contribute to the well-being of the communities in which they must live, grow, and compete.

Community-based learning emphasizing art and artlike experiences is addressed in both theory and practice in this book. Peter London has drawn on several sources to place art instruction in an educational posture that is timeless in its value and timely in its need. Significantly, he draws on over two decades of personal experience developing and testing highly effective community-based instructional strategies. The work is further informed by the reasoning of widely recognized authorities within the fields of education, psychology, philosophy, sociology, and the visual arts. Finally, his work with his students—who are, after all, a teacher's primary source of information—verifies the importance of the case he makes for community-based art education.

While explaining that "a community is not simply a conglomeration of people and places" but "also involves a pattern of interaction," London takes great care to place the student, whether very young or entering adulthood, at the center of community-based educational theory and practice. In a narrative enhanced with word mosaics, he articulates a vision of learners that honors their developmental imperatives and yet gives fair due to the adult-centered requirements of the culture into which they are being inducted. His articulation of the developmental flow that the very young enter as they begin their journey to master themselves and establish their place in a family, neighborhood, community, nation—and ultimately the world—is a welcome addition to the literature of the field of art education. It is a long-overdue reminder of what the great teachers have historically understood to be the purpose of schooling.

Continuing his emphasis on the needs of students, London contends that relevant—and thus effective—teaching begins with the knowledge and curiosity a student brings to a classroom—or more aptly, a learning place. He then identifies the community as the source of much of this knowing and discusses many rewards a community-based approach to instruction provides both teacher and learner: such an approach makes curriculums more relevant to student needs, it accelerates personal and group development, it strengthens the sensory capacities of all learners, it expands subject matter, and it informs advocacy initiatives. Clearly, the rewards are great, and they call for curricular practices that ensure their receipt.

After making a convincing case for community-based art curriculums, London outlines a wide range of instructional strategies teachers can adopt, modify, and/or amplify to implement such programs of study. In describing lessons focusing on a school yard, a city block, a five-minute walk, a vacant lot, fences, doorways, he tells and shows how teachers can lead students on a "visual odyssey" beyond the classroom, one pragmatic in its route yet exceptionally stimulating and productive in its destination.

Throughout this book, readers are not only urged to consider a most natural and effective approach to educational practice, they are compelled to reflect on their own creative development and learning styles. As the narrative unfolds and the illustrations accrue, readers are led through a refreshing examination of self and others in a manner that is truly humane, downright sensible, and long needed. And beware: if you respond to the author's invitation to "step outside," you will find it difficult to return to the secondhand world that characterizes the majority of today's classrooms.

DAVID W. BAKER
Professor of Art and Head/Art Education
University of Wisconsin–Milwaukee

This book is intended for all those who were originally drawn to art—
and to teaching art—for the satisfaction of creating expressive metaphors
that captured the thoughts and emotions evoked by firsthand encounters
with this fractious, precious world. Their motivation encompassed the
desire to enable others to partake in those same experiences and, in a way
difficult to rationalize, by so doing to save the world. As naive perhaps
as it may now seem, they believed that if only people could see how
intricate and exquisitely made the world was, they would treat it and
themselves and each other more gently, more respectfully—a terribly
romantic and improbable notion, but that was how they saw it and it gave
them strength.

This book is intended for art teachers who are still animated by a
sense of social responsibility, who know that artists require community
and that communities without artists are barren arenas indeed. They
recognize the necessary relationship between the artist and society and
wish to acknowledge it in their art teaching.

This book is intended for teachers who find themselves confined by
a curriculum irrelevant to the needs and realities of their students and who
realize that without communitywide support for their efforts, their instruction will bear little fruit. The principles for making the curriculum more
responsive to the world of the child and broadening the arena of education
to include the people, places, and events of the entire community—core

principles of community-based art education—are as applicable to any classroom as they are to the art program.

This book is intended for teachers who, confronted as they may be by the unyielding realities of inadequate resources and the well-known lists of things that make a teacher's lot an only sometimes happy one, nonetheless wish to reaffirm their faith in their earlier convictions and are determined to incorporate them into their teaching practices.

Several further observations about learning, creativity, and community underlie community-based art education. They are simply stated:

- All creative persons know what well-meaning parents, clergy, and teachers seem reluctant to accept: there are no substitutes for direct encounters with the real world. It is in wrestling with the wonders and uncertainties of life that we come to know it and love it most. From this direct knowledge and care, imagination springs and a concern for the well-made thing is born. Community-based art education offers those art teachers who feel their practice becoming tame and remote—remote from the invigorating hurly-burly of squiggly children with fresh minds engaging with bumpy but beautiful life and telling their story clear and straight—a way to revitalize their professional lives.

- We learn best when what we wish to learn and become is supported by the significant people in our lives, our family, friends, and teachers. The opposite is equally and cruelly true: we are thwarted in our learning and our becoming when the significant people in our lives are indifferent to our agenda. Learning is enabled by an intact community and hindered by its absence.

- A corollary to the above: teachers can't do it alone and schools can't do it alone, "it" being to bring about effective education, education that actually leads each new generation to wisdom and civility. As Martin Luther King, Jr., observed, we will either learn to live together as brothers (and sisters) or die together as fools. The essential partners in effective education are children, their parents, teachers, administrators, and local citizens. That's the team. If any member is missing, the whole effort suffers. The approach to teaching in this book is based squarely on the unescapable truth of this observation.

- And finally this: the world outside the classroom is far grander, more compelling, and ultimately more instructive than the world inside the classroom. To confine the resources of the teacher only to what can be found in the classroom is to shrink the curriculum and hobble both teacher and learner.

These rather obvious observations would seem to be determining factors in the design of our schools, certainly in the practice of art education. But they rarely are.

If this is a time in your career when you are seeking deeper, more consequential engagements with your students, your colleagues, your community, and the times, please read on.

Acknowledgments

If this book is to have the intended effect, it will do so because what it offers is within the resources and skills of every art teacher and every student in any school and teaching environment. I have no formal training in photography, and I took all my photos using a hand-held camera. The film was developed and printed by James Collins, then a student at the University of Massachusetts, Dartmouth.

Nothing photographed was more than a ten-minute walk from a school, and everything was photographed using existing light. No filters, tripods, cable releases, telephoto lenses, or special printing or developing processes were employed. The camera I used, a Nikkormat body combined with a Nikkor fifty-five-millimeter macro lens, approximated the range of human vision. The film was almost exclusively Kodak Tri-X ASA 400.

All my photographs were taken while walking along at street level. I didn't use step ladders, I didn't shoot from the tops of buildings, I didn't go into any buildings. No special permission was needed for any of the locations. A strong effort was made to avoid the fortuitous and unique photograph. Spectacular or high art forms were also avoided to demonstrate the ubiquity of visual resources in all areas of every community.

All the other photographs come from art teachers who employed the community-based approach to art education in their art programs. Their photographs of students at work and of the students' artwork are an essential part of this book, and I am deeply appreciative of their contributions. Thank you to:

- Sally Allan of Dover, New Hampshire, for her fourth-grade art class's splendid mural, "Our Town."

- William Allan of Brockton High School, Brockton, Massachusetts, for his creative interpretations of the "Who Goes There?" "Architectural Renderings," and "My City, My Self" projects.

- Carol Beard of the Franklin, Massachusetts, Middle School for her students' one-hundred-foot scavenger hunt.

- Gail Christie of Strong Middle School, Strong, Connecticut, for "Architectural Renderings."

- Carol Duby of the Westport, Massachusetts, elementary schools for her daughter's fine photographs, which capture children's outdoor sketching and the artwork they produced, "Our Court Yard."

- Peter Geisser for his insightful work with students of the Rhode Island School for the Deaf, Providence, Rhode Island, and in particular for the "Trojan Horse," "Oriental Rugs," "Children's

Hospital Clay Tile," and "Lion Gate" projects, undertaken in and around the Rhode Island School for the Deaf building.

- Betsy Hubner of Burr and Burton Seminary, Manchester, Vermont, for her students' thoughtful and sensitive pieces, "Boxes of Myself," using found objects.

- Helen Potter of the Billerica, Massachusetts, school system for the joyous work from the children in her elementary art classes: "Our Playground," "Fantastic Found Objects," "Iggy the Lizard," "Icky Bugs," and "Landscapes."

- Joan L'Homme of Pulaski Elementary School in New Bedford, Massachusetts, for her enthusiasm for teaching and for her students' exuberant projects represented here: the "My Town" mural, "My Self/My Flowers," "Circus Clowns," "My Pet," "Neighborhood Stores," "Snow Storm," "Community Store Fronts," "My Family, My House," "My Favorite Room," "Springtime," and "Bugs, Flowers, Planes."

- Kathy Miraglia of Friends Academy, North Dartmouth, Massachusetts, for the "Found Objects," self-portraits, and autobiographic stabiles of her elementary art classes.

- Ann Schauman of Rochester, New York, Middle School for her innovative work with inner-city children: "Rochester's Public Art," "Masking Traditions, Personal Masking," and "Doorways of Pride."

- Melissa Smith of the Fall River, Massachusetts, elementary schools for her children's "Fences" artworks.

- Jean Staiti, Director of Art for the Fall River schools, for "Crafted with Pride in Fall River."

STEP
OUT-
SIDE

1 Seeing for Ourselves

Artistic expression is born from personal experience. To the degree that one's personal encounters with the world are engaging and vivid, one will discover material for engaging and vivid personal expression. Such experiences need not be heroic or even very dramatic, but they do need to be personally and carefully encountered. Secondhand accounts of someone else's impressions of yet someone else's deeds conveyed through sign and symbol offer a diluted, generalized, and distorted rendition of nature's fullness. The learner's personal experience—and the art produced from this vicarious contact—is also likely to be diluted, generalized, and distorted.

The arts, whether visual, literary, or performing, are richer in meaning when they are an expression of experiences that matter deeply. Things and events that matter, that have the potential to shape people's lives, take place within the immediate environment or community. The community is the place where friends are made and enemies are grappled with. It is here that dreams and fantasies are generated and tested, where the triumphs and the tearful losses of life are encountered. The community is the web of life that inextricably embraces, defines, and empowers children and adults alike. Using the school as its base of operations, community-based art education forays out into the community for its motivation and its subject matter. The community is the arena for the creative expression of personal encounters with one's environment, one's web of life.

It is ironic that in today's schools, which depend increasingly on expensive audiovisual equipment to bring secondhand news about the outside world into the classroom, there exists a fine device that is rarely used to its full advantage—the *door*. This simple apparatus allows students to step outside and encounter a world far richer than the reduced and predigested shadow-of-the-world our schools offer in its stead.

Within a radius of thirty feet, only twenty *seconds* away from the front door of any school, may be found growing green grass; shiny, tiny orange-and-black lady bugs; glittery silver foil; sheets of metal (in the form of cans or cars); smooth and rough pebbles and rocks; sinewy weeds; springs, bottle tops, and nails; coffee-colored newspapers; shiny, rusty, red, blue, green automobile parts; squeaks, shouts, bells, and roars; rustling, scuffing, and tapping; black, pink, yellow, brown, red people; little girls and boys in sneakers; mothers with babies; cats and dogs; clouds, blue-yellow-green mottled skies; wind in the trees and in the clothes and in the hair; letters, words, designs; shingles, peeled paint, red fences; brown and orange and red and black dirt; stuff between the cracks in the sidewalk; heat, cool shade. All this at the very portal of the school. Imagine the riches just behind that house or around that corner or on the other side of that door or in that vegetable market or in that vacant lot. And the people! All those experts flowing past the school, never asked to share their store of knowledge with the younger generation, what they know about the qual-

ities of rubber, finding a ripe melon, what happened in Dieppe during the invasion, how to catch a trout, the easiest way to get to Brockville, why turnips have to be cooked, or how to tie a hawser, clean a fish, fix cars, build boats, calculate, cook, mend, measure, govern, remember, imagine, hope.

Once a year the school's portals open to admit a small group of uncertain, wide-eyed youngsters. In buildings like this, for the next ten to twenty years, these children will spend some fifteen thousand hours away from the raw, always surprising, endlessly fascinating world, reading and listening to adults "preparing" them for a life they in fact will never experience. Extracted from streets full of old people, young people, dreamers, shoppers; from telling stories, choosing sides, running, screaming, kissing, fighting, scheming, playing, growing, learning, the squirming youth of the world are brushed, combed, and cleaned into place in the hope they will return to that world equipped not merely to cope but to change it for the better.

In the midst of the seething, swarming mass of people, places, things, that constitute the rich, loamy soil of the community, special areas are cleared of this cultural debris. Here brick, glass, and steel are put together to form a school, a protective enclave far from harm's way. Here, behind doors, behind desks, sit children, looking at pictures and reading texts about what is going on outside. Not party to the democratic processes, the children are taught *about* democracy. Extracted from the daily necessities of coping with life's situations, they are taught *about* social studies and current events. Far from the spontaneity that causes people to love, sing, dance, and laugh, they are taught dance steps, words to songs, and the proper ways of greeting.

With desks geometrically arranged, with bells that ring at set intervals signaling the end of one "experience" and the beginning of another, with adults patrolling the hallways, stairways, lunchrooms, bathrooms, playgrounds, and buses, schools monitor the behavior of children lest they evidence not only waywardness but, all too often, the malady called "carefree youth." Scraped and washed free of all the chewing gum and dirty elbows, of the seeking and the give-and-take learning of the streets, the innately curious child, whom Buckminster Fuller calls the first and real scientific investigator, becomes a student.

Little space is provided for spontaneity or privacy. Children study books *about* Magellan, Vasco da Gama, and Marco Polo; books *about* the Nile, the Congo, and the Tigris-Euphrates; pictures *of* the Parthenon, Stonehenge, and Machu Picchu—other people's revelations, investigations, analyses, passions, and tragedies. The children's own experiences with their wide, exhilarating, mysterious world will have to wait. The daring, the trials and errors, and the idiosyncrasies lauded in others are scarcely tolerated here, since such behavior might disturb the class or

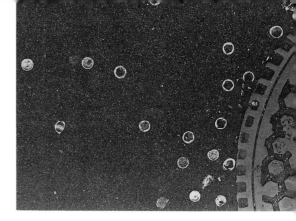

keep it from completing the assignment on the French Revolution before the end of the month, when the next chapter of the text must be begun.

For those who will not or cannot easily be separated from their bag of bottle caps, stuffed animals, baseball cards, silver foil balls, dolls, and ribbons, or pulled away from the teasing, gossiping, meeting, choosing, poking, and giggling of the streets, school is hard, and their teachers are pressed. Some children, whose street ways are resistant to teacher conferences, grades, and parent meetings, require detention or suspension. An ironic punishment: exile to the streets, the same streets these incorrigibles so desperately wish to return to. Those that can be made to set aside their passions, their derring-do, their playfulness, their spontaneity, who can abide the demand to be an obliging student rather than a searching, active human being, supply the schools with their most workable and rewarding material.

The cornucopia of life heaps together—without discrimination or preordained order—puddles and pavement, friends and enemies, rubber bands and lady bugs. Children swim through this thick soup every day on their way to school. Once they are safely inside, schools provide them with words in a line, picture stories of other people's adventures, accounts of other people's discoveries, three-by-five-inch black-and-white photos on thin paper as a substitute for the experience of encountering a snail crossing a leaf or an elderly lady who remembers the day her son went off to war. Replacing the incredible amount and kind of edibles children find to satisfy their need to snack, the school, when it has the wherewithal to provide refreshment of any kind, instead offers milk (to be sipped with a straw, no noise at the bottom, please) and plain cookies (please, no fudge, no filling, no nuts, no double-deckers, no marshmallow, no crumbly fancy stuff, no oversized or iced cookies, please!).

In place of encounters with child-scale events that emerge from the actual life of the child, schoolchildren are required to listen to an adult talk and write about the exploits of adults. Adult-satisfying manners, adult-designed single-concept film loops, managed texts, circumscribed histories, colorless language, and predictable homework assignments (more often than not about other times and other places) soon crowd out the natural work of childhood and the inquiring mind and hands of the child. Compelled to devote their energies to ingesting someone else's conclusions about the pattern and movement of life, children frequently fail to develop their own capacities.

Every time children have a firsthand encounter with life and with one another, real tasks and real problem solving of necessity arise. When even the youngest of children get together to play—at building castles in the sand, for instance—they have to execute a series of subtle and complex acts of mind. First, they have to focus their attention on a significant aspect of the seamless envelope of people, places, things, and events that

surround them—the ownership of one of the shovels, for example. Then they must form relationships between the phenomena they observe and appropriate past or parallel phenomena: who brought the shovel, who was using it last, what rights does the current user have over the prior user, and so on. Following this, they have to recognize the implications of the relationship between what they presently have and what they desire: Sara wants the shovel, but so do Michael and Alice; Bill is using it now, but Randy hasn't had a chance to use it yet. Then they must design a course of action in the light of these anticipated implications: give it back to Sara, or give it to Randy now and then give it to Sara, trade Bill the rake for the shovel, and so on. This done, they must judge the worth of each alternative in the light of their previous experience and then decide to act upon a selected alternative: if we give it to Randy, then Sara will start crying and Bill will hit Randy; if we give it back to Sara, then. . . . Now they must initiate the necessary steps to execute the decision, constantly checking back to prior operations to ensure the validity of each step. Okay, who is in favor of giving the shovel to Sara? Sara, put that rake down, Clive, get back in here! Finally, they must evaluate the outcome in light of the immediately preceding and all previous analogous experience.

Contrast this with a sketch of the operations necessary to succeed in the tasks that schools most often demand of students, such as, read the

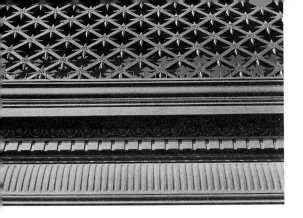

chapter on Vasco da Gama and answer questions 1, 3, 5, and 7. Spelling counts! In this case, children must first accept a task imposed by someone who is not a peer. Then they must read the material and memorize as much of that material as they can. Following this, they must read and comprehend the given rules of problem solving and then apply them to the organized questions the author of the text felt were most important. Then they must respond to these preset questions according to preset rules of acceptable form and submit the results of this activity to an outside authority (the teacher) for evaluation. Finally, in all but the rarest cases of student self-assertion, they are required to accept the evaluation of their efforts by this same outside authority.

Thus, not only does schooling often substitute secondhand experience for raw reality, it also fosters a passive intellect through a school day composed of adult-designed, prearranged problems that neither emerge from nor relate back to the actual lives of children.

As they progress through their school years, young people become convinced that the news media are more substantial, more legitimate, than their own experience. They learn to dismiss and distrust their own instincts and their own perceptions. Often, the children who are successful in school are those for whom the acceptance of rules, norms, and canons of good form is more compelling than dealing with the messy stuff of everyday life. They achieve an A in math, but can they balance their

checkbook? They get an A in history, but are they active and informed citizens? They get an A in art, but do they pick up a brush with confidence and joy after graduation? They learn about pollution, but do they work with their family and neighborhood to recycle? They learn about poverty and the homeless, but do they volunteer time in the local soup kitchen? They learn about addictions, but do they turn in or against their peers who are users or pushers? Hard to say.

Why should the curriculum primarily consist of predigested material? Why not invigorate it by using the real, live, pulsating community as the supply closet, the visual aids department, the resource center, the guest lecture series, the periodical guide, the living textbook center, the special effects department of the school? And why not use the classroom for seminars, tutorials, reading, studio work, inquiry, displays, and performances to complement the input obtained from outside the school building?

Vacant lots, parks, farmers' markets, fabric houses, record stores, upholstery shops, garages, frame shops, flower shops; bakers, painters, accountants, bankers, foundry workers, plumbers, printers, masons, pipe fitters; children running, jumping, hiding, scheming, climbing, reading, stretching, learning, learning, learning. It's all right there, right outside. Why not step outside?

Firsthand Experience

Most schooling is accomplished by means of explanation and symbolic representation of life. Through worksheets, kits, slides, books, tapes, movies, pictures, lectures, and so on, schools attempt to convey to students the "facts" about life. Art programs are no different, for they too use these devices to explain and motivate. Yet there is a great discrepancy between firsthand experience and its symbolic representation, as much difference as between eating a cool, juicy peach on a hot summer day and looking at the label on a can of sliced peaches.

The approach to art education taken here begins with firsthand experience of the immediate world, and thus it offers educational rewards not easily achieved by vicarious means. Direct experience of the environment differs from vicarious accounts in several important ways. Direct experience brings the participant into contact with the thing itself in all its color, texture, dynamics, and raw otherness. Confronting the natural world directly has a degree of unexpectedness, of uncertainty about what is going to happen next. This dramatic sense of expectancy in facing the unpredictable, unfolding world is absent from secondhand encounters. It's like playing a game of baseball instead of watching a videotape of last year's World Series on a VCR. The unfolding quality of nature requires an active mind to perceive, analyze, and organize the experience into coherent and relevant information. Vicarious information is already pre-

selected and packaged, contains no further surprises. All it requires is our passive acceptance.

Art programs based primarily on vicarious experience constrict these vital intellectual and sensorial activities by providing predigested motivation and predetermined problem-setting and problem-solving procedures. Ultimately, it matters very little if we are successful in looking at slides and identifying artist, date, style, and title. In truth, it also matters very little how finely wrought our pictures are. What matters mightily, however, is whether or not we are successful at organizing and making sense of our world and at forming our experience into works that enhance the quality of our life and that of the community.

The main work of the creative person—and the main reward of a creative arts program—is to be able to look at the world with wonder and awe, to be able to direct attention to the richest, most significant parts of the world, to ask the most penetrating questions, to design the most effective strategies for accomplishing goals, and to create the most significant symbols to represent the experience.

Any art worth attending to conveys the sense that the artist had an experience that made such a deep impression, the imprint of that original experience is still evident in the work. This sense of actually having been there, of having grappled with something, is evidenced in the peculiarly apt employment of color, form, and line, in the vivacity and surety of

technique, and in the evocative nature of the work's composition and imagery. Art produced from hearsay all too often has a certain predictability and staleness, a vagueness, a lackluster aura.

To illustrate what a community-based art program would look like in practice, I offer two examples. One takes place in an elementary school in a small town, the other in a large high school in a city. Both schools consist of the full complement of class personalities and abilities, and both have art periods of thirty to fifty minutes one to three times a week, a typical situation for millions of children and their teachers.

The art projects these two schools undertook are designed to be uncomplicated and require only basic skills. They are easy projects for any student and any teacher in any school in almost any community. They exemplify many of the traits to be described in greater detail later in the text. Each attempts to demonstrate how the community can be explored, how it can be used as a source of relevant creative expression, and how it can generate learning. These are not full lesson plans but only a basic outline of the activities.

Take One Hundred Steps

Bringing a third-grade class to the front door of the school, the teacher takes a hundred-foot ball of string, fastens one end to the doorknob, gives the ball of string to a child, and asks the child to walk away from the

school to the end of the string. The child then walks in an arc with a hundred-foot radius, delineating this path with string from another ball. This half-moon hunting ground may encompass lawn, shrubs, sidewalks, streets, and curbs. Equipped with paper bags, each child scours the range and secures an example of everything that is not toxic or private property and that will fit inside the circle of thumb and index fingers. They are utter vacuum cleaners, leaving no stone unturned.

Their bags stuffed with the artifacts of local life, the children return to the classroom and dump out their gleanings. First, they simply share the surprises of their myriad findings. Next, they sort the items according to color from shades of dark to light or warm to cool (or according to material, usage, shape, etc.). Equipped now with a huge palette of hues, tones, and textures, the children recombine these small samples of their immediate vicinity to create a mural-size collage expressive of the community as it looks or as it feels to live in. Or, using the material directly as a tactile and visual expression, they create an abstraction that expresses the beat and rhythm of the neighborhood. When the piece is completed, they consider where the piece will be installed. Possible sites are the community center, the library, a bank lobby, the mayor's office, the recreation hall of the Senior Citizens Center, or their school cafeteria.

Who Goes There?

In this lesson another simple idea, texture rubbings, is used to demonstrate the concepts of curriculum design offered in a community-based art program. Conducted in an urban high school, the project includes team efforts, interdisciplinary studies, and a great deal of interaction with the community.

An old three-story brick school building shares a crowded block with apartment houses, small stores, a parking lot, and many different people and types of vehicles. The buildings represent a dozen different styles of architecture and as many different personal tastes. The people represent many ethnic backgrounds. Who are these people? Where are they going? What clues can we gather about their daily activities?

The art and social studies teachers conduct this lesson, having previously worked together introducing their students to the idea that geography influences architecture. This art project explores the idea that cities owe their vigor and their abrasive qualities to the diversity of people incessantly mingling among one another. Both teachers lead their tenth-grade classes to the front door of the school, where the students, working in teams of three, set out on a hundred-foot exploration of patterns of movement in this section of their community. Each team has previously

discussed and selected a site with a particular kind of traffic flow and now tapes a long sheet of newsprint to the sidewalk there. The sites chosen include the entrance to the school and the entrances to a candy store, restaurant, and bank. The normal grime of a city provides the "ink." (For a better print, a sheet of charcoaled paper can be sandwiched face up between sidewalk and newsprint.) The pressure of feet and vehicles against the texture of the ground supplies the necessary pressure for contact prints. The students also make quick gesture and character sketches of the people passing over their prints. After a "press run" of ten minutes, the papers are lifted and brought back to the art classroom, pinned up, and briefly reviewed before the end of the class period. It is clear that some areas received more traffic than others and even that different types of shoes were worn by the people using the various institutions.

The next day, the students look more carefully at the materials and decide how to proceed with the work. Along with their teachers they derive a number of possible projects and settle on the following idea: to illustrate the point that their neighborhood actually consists of a number of different types of institutions, each with its own clientele, that the neighborhood is more like a patchwork quilt than a single, homogeneous entity. After discussing these factors and how they affect their lives, the students explore how they might express all this visually. A number of sketches and further discussions enable them to decide on a strategy.

The original prints are blown up, and their soft tones become the background for a series of megamurals. Superimposed on this background are outline paintings of the buildings and their clientele derived from the gesture drawings the students made on site. With the permission of the administration and the janitors' okay, these megamurals are then installed as a frieze along the outside of the building, enhancing the neighborhood and indicating that this school is part of and aware of its place in the community.

Meeting the Tiger: Four Views

Community-based art education begins where learning theory and psychology tell us *all* learning begins: with *experience*, with direct encounters with life. The important distinction between having an experience and observing an account of someone else's experience—and the different kinds of learning that result—may be made clearer through another series of illustrations. These examples demonstrate that both the subject and the object of the experience are mutually transformed by the encounter and that the same partners take on entirely different qualities under different degrees of engagement. They also show that firsthand experience is much more meaningful and emotionally rich than vicarious contact and nature much more awesome than its representations. Our examples center on an animal that is the subject of much art and myth: the tiger.

I

Imagine first, an encounter with a tiger in the animal's natural habitat. In the heat of midday, tall, dry grasses rustle in the faint breeze, the dark green jungle a wall behind them. Then, what seems to be only the shadow of the grasses suddenly melts into a shape—could it be?—a tiger! We are shocked by her actual size and color and lethal grace. As she glides back into the bush, our knees go weak with the aftershock. Except for the pounding of our heart, the jungle seems to have shut down, fallen silent. Then, a heavy cough fills the clearing and she appears again, this time much closer. The sunlight on her orange-black-white coat makes this queen of death strangely more handsome and graceful than we had thought. Again she coughs. Seeing us, she freezes, lowers her head, bunching muscles all along her shoulders. Black lips curling back expose many sharp yellow teeth. Wet mouth drawn back, target eyes unblinking, she deliberately coughs one final time before launching herself toward us.

II

Our next encounter with the tiger is in a zoo, but this time we are on opposite sides of iron bars. A knot of people squeezes together and hoots in front of one of the cages. Working our way through craning necks, falsetto counterfeit roars, and popcorn offerings, we finally glimpse the caged beast. Head held loose, remarkably narrow of hip, he mechanically

paces his tiny domain. His claws, filed down to harmless stubs from endless pacing, make light metallic sounds, like the ticking of a mindless clock. The popcorn thrown his way is hardly the meal he has in mind and doesn't interrupt his gaze or his pacing. The tiger is the only silent member of this crowd. Parents holding kids eating ice cream stand within a claw's strike. But the animal makes no attempt to swat them away. Soon he urinates on the concrete, settles stiffly in a far corner, and closes his eyes, his back to the crowd. The mighty beast at rest. The moms and dads and kids move on to another cage, where the gazelles are now gathering for their noonday meal: a healthy blend of nutritionally fortified food pellets.

III

The tiger next appears in the social studies classroom through the magic of an audiovisual presentation. Following the spelling test (today's words include *India, jungle, tiger, Hindu*), the room is darkened and the teacher continues the unit "India, The West's Democratic Experiment in Asia." Somewhere in between images of Gandhi, Nehru, the docks of Calcutta, and turbaned Sikhs, there are two slides of tigers, one standing majestic against the golden grasses, forever motionless and silent, the other a pelt splayed out on the wall of a raja's palace, also forever motionless and silent but this time with the head frozen in a perpetual snarl. The children's geography textbook also has a section on tigers—well, one picture of a

tigress and her cubs. The three-by-five-inch photograph is in black and white. The caption underneath says that there are only 6,233 of these majestic beasts left in the entire world.

IV

Finally, children meet up with the beast in the art classroom. The setting is quite lovely: Chagall prints of fantasy Russian villages and a photograph of the *Pièta* by Michelangelo, each appropriately labeled and framed with construction paper, hang on the wall, and some egg-carton mobiles à la Calder swing gaily overhead. After taking attendance and signing some late passes, the teacher "motivates" the children by asking them to remember their last visit to the zoo, probing them for their opinion about which was the most awesome and majestic animal. Discarding responses of elephants, rhinos, and gorillas, the teacher winnows her way to the desired answer, the tiger. Reinforcing the motivation, the teacher also shows the class some *National Geographic* pictures on the overhead projector and some Chinese ink drawings of tigers (or are they snow leopards?). Handing out bright orange construction paper, black crayons, and scissors, she asks the class to design a poster on saving endangered animals using the figure of the tiger as the main motif and paying particular attention to line quality and contrast.

Notice how the image of the tiger changes in each environment—from a powerful and untamed force, to a listless and indifferent object, to some black-and-white dots on paper, and finally to orange paper and black crayon. Notice, too, how the observer changes—from an awestruck potential victim, to a gawking onlooker, to a distracted social studies student, and finally to a poster maker executing an assigned project according to someone else's values.

Not Another Field Trip!

Community-based art education, like any experiential learning, invites a close working relationship between school and community. However, when teachers think of expanding their curriculum and forum to include elements of the "real" world, they usually turn to the conventional field trip. Most teachers who avail themselves of this venerable means know all too well the trouble it is and the dubious rewards it offers. Egg salad and peanut-butter-and-jelly sandwiches smeared on bus windows and squished underfoot, spilt milk, nausea, insipid chanting, head counts, and lost money, books, and kids are only a small part of the price most teachers pay for taking their students on a field trip. Regardless of the planning, permission slips, parent helpers, preliminary lessons, and home-work assignments, field trips are for most children a holiday from the

routines and confinement of the classroom. These forays out of school all too often place the student in the role of a mischievous kid surrounded by slaphappy cronies who all somehow got passes to the bathroom at the same time.

Field trips needn't be the frantic and exhausting experiences they too often turn out to be, but for some basic structural reasons inherent in the method of instruction of the entire curriculum, they usually are just that. For one thing, they provide no real engagement with the raw world, no problem to raise or mitigate or solve—at least none intended by the teacher. Although the trip is carried out in the real world, the children are usually hurried through the community to the designated site. Any casual engagement with the community on the way to and from the designated site is grounds for reprimand or worse. Most field trips involve taking a group of students to observe something that has happened many times before and will happen many times again in just the same way, regardless of the presence or absence of the children. The same bemused audience is simply being carted off to another park or playground or zoo or museum. As rich and carefully constructed to maximize learning as these sites are, they are all shaped and managed to provide an object lesson or performance with a predetermined meaning and emphasis. And field trips are usually only illustrative of a subject already studied or about to be studied.

Experiential, community-based art programs differ from field trips in the same way that encounters with tigers in jungles differ from encounters with tigers in zoos. In community-based art education, the child's encounter with a real but focused aspect of the environment provides the initiating context for a genuine meeting between the inherently curious mind of the child and the even more curious world. The kind of engagement with the community advocated here expands upon the general idea of a field trip by advocating field research, interviews, sample taking, mapping, documenting, measuring, comparing, drawing, and recording firsthand impressions. Then, back in the classroom, the children and teacher can extract the educational rewards of their experiences by analyzing their findings and synthesizing them into meaningful statements and personal expressions, noticing which observations are shared, which are unique, and moving on to questions about the sources of objectivity and the proper domain of subjectivity, about accuracy, opinion, and truth. What is truth, and how do we know it?

2 What's in It for Them (And Us)?

To acknowledge the value of firsthand encounters with the world as evocative foundations for learning in general and creative expression in particular is one thing. But public school curriculums must address the pressing requirements of these educational times: they must be relevant for the learners; they must be sensitive to students of all backgrounds, learning styles, and interests; they must attend to both the cognitive and the affective domain; they must be cost effective; and they must establish positive working relations with the community. Community-based art education more than meets these challenges.

It Is Inherently Artistic

Any worthwhile art education proposal must be based on how artists think and what they do, and community-based art education is based on precisely that. Artists' distinctive quality of mind is that *they see for themselves.* Their whole stance to life, what fuels their creativity, is their insistence upon engaging with life directly and making up their own minds about what is of value and what needs improvement. Like scientists and intellectually courageous people in any discipline, artists require direct access to the world; secondhand sources are inadequate. They need to encounter the raw material. Through this unmitigated contact with the world, artists enjoy the pleasure of witnessing the world as if for the first time. This is why their work has freshness and vitality and why the viewer also has the refreshing experience of seeing traditional themes and objects as if for the first time.

Conventional education—and art education is no exception—presents students with secondhand replications of the world. Community-based art education presents students with the opportunity to engage life directly, and not simply life in general, but precisely that part that is central to the life of the child, the community.

The great task of the artist, of any artistic person, is to approach the welter of things in the world and to select those that resonate for them with particular poignancy. The community-based approach to art education provides for such opportunities by bringing children into direct contact with the world, then allowing each child to discover the particular connection she or he finds most relevant. Community-based art education does not bring children back into their own community only to say, See the handsome facade of that building? Try to capture it using only contour line. Instead, this approach brings the children into the midst of their world and says, We were just talking about how some buildings seem to welcome you, while others make you feel you don't want to go in. Walk along this block and find examples of ones that welcome you and ones that repel you. Using appropriate material, create images not only of what you see but of how you feel about it.

In this way, community-based art education allows the force of the

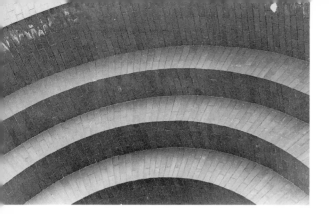

encounter between children and their world to determine the eventual form their artistic expression will take. Unlike most art education practice, which designs lessons that already have in mind an eventual look and form for the children's activity, community-based art education has no particular end product in mind. It trusts that authentic encounters with the world will provide the necessary impetus and focus for children to *desire* a personal and creative response. Viktor Lowenfeld, in his landmark book *Creative and Mental Growth,* lays down tenets for employing the creative process in art education that community-based art education respectfully acknowledges and embraces. He observes that children's self-expression is richest and most meaningful *for* them when the subject matter is most meaningful *to* them and they are free to express themselves in self-appropriated ways. Lowenfeld constantly reminds art teachers to ask themselves, What is of interest to *this* child, here and now? Imposing adult themes on a child and adult means of expression on a child's mind is not simply ineffective, it is positively destructive of our whole ambition, which is not to make art, but through the creative process to nurture creative and mental growth.

Community-based art education thinks and proceeds likewise. It starts with the children's world, their community, provides firsthand encounters with it, and allows children to express their reactions to their world in expressive forms congenial to their thinking. This is an unabashedly

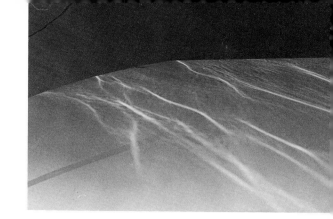

humanistic, child-centered pedagogy. It is exactly what artists and all original, inquiring minds do. The artist's studio is *not* animated by lessons imposed by others! The artist's studio is characterized by creative responses to a "witnessing" of some aspect of this stunning world. Community-based art education does this too.

It Begins with Students' Knowledge and Curiosity

Who was Piero della Francesca? How do you multiply fractions? How do you say thank you in Spanish? When did Magellan discover the Pacific Ocean? Matters like these confront students every day, presenting them with questions they frequently do not know the answer to—nor do they know how to verify someone else's answer. (Just as frequently, they don't care very much what the answer is anyway.) An overarching sense of inferiority and ignorance of the adult world permeates our schooling, a high price for children to pay for this teaching method. Its common practice makes it seem that these consequences are the natural and necessary price for acquiring new skills and knowledge. And yet one can be led to increased experience and knowledge without paying this price, in the quite simple and natural way John Dewey and the Progressive Education movement so adequately described and demonstrated. John Dewey's *Schools of Tomorrow*, Hughes Mearns's *Creative Power*, and the writings of Thomas L. Hopkins, Paul Goodman, E. L. Thorndike, and Carl Rogers

are instructive here. This view of education begins from where the child literally is, where his curiosities are, where she lives and plays, where he has labyrinths of secret hiding places, how she shapes her archetypal images, the stuff of his dreams. Inquiring first what children know and care about, then what *their* questions are, about what *they* wish to know more, the experiential curriculum offers further explorations in these directions and in related domains not yet encountered or often even imagined by the child. In this fashion, the student moves from the familiar to the new, always working from a sense of personal orientation and perspective, and with an unfolding, organic sequence of issues and discoveries.

32

It Is Relevant

What issue or subject could be more relevant to the learner than the nature of oneself and one's world at this time and in this place? This experiential art program starts with plotting the map of oneself and of the landscape one treads daily. In as much as Who am I? Where am I? and How can I go from where I am to where I want to be? are relevant questions, this program is relevant. Students investigate other people's experiences and settings to seek parallels and contrasts that confirm and expand the quality of their own personal perceptions and expressions.

Like the entire human species, the child has an insatiable desire to

know more and do better. The constant shower of intriguing information that living brings can't help but promote children's appetite for ever more extensive engagements with their world. This drive for increasing experience assures us that although the curriculum starts with the self, the expanding self will not be satisfied with peering at itself alone; it will naturally expand toward other relevant associations: the family, neighborhood, community, nation, world. This is the basic observation Viktor Lowenfeld makes in *Creative and Mental Growth*. It is the central feature of this approach to art education as well.

It Is Contemporary

Beginning as it does with the here and now rather than with someone else's there and then, this program is based on the notion that a historical perspective and an appreciation of history are most effectively derived from an initial sense of self in the immediate environment. From the study of the personal environment, the child's *natural* curiosity, guided by the teacher, proceeds in ever-widening circles of experience, noticing both the antecedents and the implications. Children in this program can be likened to investigative reporters for daily newspapers, who *first* catch the essential pulse of the immediate context of which they are a part and *then* seek the causes of the event. Subsequently, they can exercise their editorial prerogatives, offering their own views on the implications of the event.

It Is Accessible

Wherever we are, whatever constitutes our web of life, is the place and the subject of study in this program. There is no more accessible place than the community in which we live. We are always in the best seats to view the drama of *our* lives. The environment, the primary subject matter of this curriculum, is always there. It is never too far to get to. We can never run out of it, and it never belongs to someone else. *The environment is us.* It is the life support system in which we are all inextricably embedded. The community is everything that touches the life of each child. It is always at hand physically, intellectually, and emotionally. This program simply makes this fact perceptible. The ever-abundant, always available, constantly new raw material of living here and now becomes the basic resource for subsequent creative expression.

It Acknowledges Concern About Safety

It is a telling criticism of our streets and neighborhoods that they are not as safe as we want them to be. Wouldn't a community-based educational system unnecessarily place students in harm's way, outside the safety zone of the school building?

There are several responses to this legitimate concern, which, I believe, only strengthen the case for community-based education. The first and most obvious one is that the schools in dangerous neighborhoods

are no less dangerous than the streets themselves. I know of no statistics that would make an exact case for this, but my thirty years as a teacher and a student of schooling and as a general reader of the news media convince me that violence in the schools is no less frequent than the violence children experience in their own neighborhoods. (I will only mention in passing the deplorable truth that the home is a place of questionable security and well-being for too many of our children.) I am not making the case for the safety of the streets. The streets, however, neighborhood by neighborhood, are probably no more nor any less safe for children than the other places they frequent.

To object to using the community as a primary educational resource for safety's sake is as justified as objecting to returning the children to their homes and their neighborhoods after school is dismissed or, for that matter, objecting to sending children to many of our schools at all.

No, there is no high ground in our society for many of our children. What we can do is to provide them with an education that promotes their survival, their very success, in the homes, streets, and neighborhoods they do inhabit. The community of the child is the only place that survival and success can occur for that child. A curriculum that ignores the child's community and studies other times and other places, with scant regard for this child's time and this child's place, prepares the child poorly for successes that matter deeply, here and now or in the future.

It can be said that streets, neighborhoods, homes, and schools are most dangerous for people who are most ignorant about them. People who know their domain, who know its resources, history, patterns, and expectations, its values and taboos, the places to avoid and those to seek out, do far better than those who do not.

Community-based art education directly addresses all the diverse issues that arise as a result of engagement in a particular community. In this way, it provides a relevant, timely, necessary curriculum in which tools for success are cultivated for the child's current life and future possibilities.

Community-based art education is not complacent about our failing neighborhoods and the growing alienation between the public schools and the public that supports them. This approach intends to improve the quality of community life and reestablish a congenial working relationship between school and community. It does this by introducing functional relationships among students, parents, teachers, and citizens so that each group is rewarded through its distinctive contributions to the common good. Thus, children are provided with a relevant curriculum, a wide network of resourceful adults, and rich material for positive and necessary engagements with the real world, all of which enable them to achieve rich aesthetic expression and a full, imaginative life.

It Is Inexpensive

No bus fares. No admission fees. No requisitions for expensive slide programs, boxes of labeled rocks, or science- or art-in-a-nutshell kits. No need for slide projectors, movie projectors, film loops, opaque overhead projectors. No lost slides, broken bulbs, ripped movie screens, blown TV tubes, absent sound, broken sprockets, torn tape. American education, like America in general, has bought into the notion that hardware and gadgets can bring knowledge and happiness. It has never worked. The wonder is why we ever fell for this elusive panacea in the first place. The most sophisticated instruments (and therefore the most expensive and fragile, and therefore the most protected and exclusive) are really sophisticated attempts to replicate, with minimal distortion, the real world. Some technology—microscopes, telescopes, potter's wheels, and computers, for example—does increase our perceptual and manipulative powers. My brief is confined to the technology that attempts to rerepresent nature and living and does it poorly. Instead of spending thousands on the newest hardware, which can only offer the merest and dimmest glimpse of a spring day, how about popping outside for five minutes and just listening, eyes shut, to the high fidelity of a spring morning or a traffic jam or rain in the alley, then going back to represent those high-fi, quadraphonic, multisensory impressions in media that are matched to the original sensations?

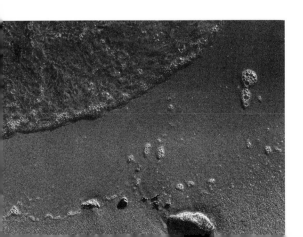

It Is Multisensory

A very nice thing about the environment is that it always comes in full, living color and high-fidelity, quadraphonic sound. It is infinitely available and inviting to touch, taste, look at, and smell.

Being always and fully multisensory, the environment kindly makes itself available to all, whatever their wealth or station in life or the limitations on their sensory capacities. Rather than being heavily dependent on facility with language and skill at oral interpretation, as schools so often are, this program offers an opportunity for all children to attend to the world, to be moved by it, and to shape it into expressive form.

In a talk given at Harvard University in the early spring of 1980, Gregory Bateson, the learning theorist and cultural anthropologist, made the revealing observation that all learning requires multisensory input. By learning, he meant experiences that lead to appropriate modified and sustained behavior, not simply the memory of things seen or heard. Bateson noted that existing behavior is extremely durable and that it often takes a critical number of different sensory inputs to confirm the validity of change and the necessity for change. Unless several different senses confirm the validity of the input, the human system rejects the information and won't act on it. Hearing is not enough, seeing is not enough, neither is touching or smelling in and of themselves. Bateson claims that at a minimum three different sense organs must each receive similar "news"

before the credibility of that news is established and we are willing to act on it.

Well, the community is inherently multisensory, and almost all items in it come to us through several senses simultaneously. The community, therefore, provides the optimal setting for learning. All children, whatever their perceptual sensitivity or insensitivity, have an opportunity to "hear the news" in this approach to education and, later, in the classroom, to consider and express their reactions in a number of modalities.

It Is Natural and Easy

This program proceeds from the proposition that the cultivation of an open mind, a wondering and careful eye, and a genuine curiosity in confronting a dense and surprising environment will generate the knowledge and skills necessary for a potentially successful and pleasurable life. Instead of the teacher alone having to provide all the questions, all the resource materials, all the motivations, all the skills, and all the answers, this program places the responsibility on the learner and the teacher. My claim is that all but the most severely impaired children have sufficient curiosity about the world. When confronted with the actual environment, the child will explore it in order to more deeply savor, understand, and employ it to his or her advantage. Children experience this approach to education as natural and easy because they are always working from what

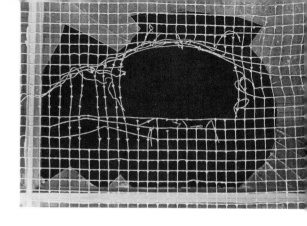

they know to what they want to know: there is no need for the usual pushing and prodding that characterize much of our current schooling. The content and the thinking required are not simple or easy, but the labor is pleasant and feels honest, and that makes the effort exhilarating. This exhilaration in learning more powerful ways to know about and succeed in the world makes education feel easy for both the teacher and the students.

It Is Interdisciplinary

In few other areas besides school is knowledge segregated into disciplines. Art, music, geography, languages, mathematics, are slices of a whole. As useful as these subjects are as a means of investigating a part of the whole, they do not in themselves offer a picture of the whole. The "whole" is the seamless web of life itself. In schools, we seldom use these disciplines to describe and analyze the environment. Instead, we simply study the disciplines themselves. We study the history and the achievements of the discipline, we study the lives of the great people of the discipline and the impact of their discoveries on other people in other times and places, and we study and commit to memory the formulas, theorems, dates, and names making up the lexicon of the discipline. Physics is the nature of nature at certain levels of interaction. But the study of the subject "physics" is *not* nature, but the study of that particular discipline of knowledge. In

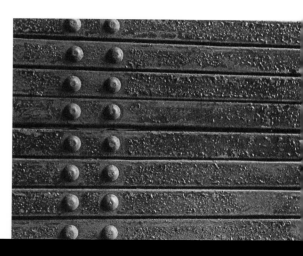

physics classes, one rarely actually times the velocity of trains or other projectiles. One studies Newton's laws and learns that mass times velocity equals force (of impact), yet one still doesn't fasten the seat belt during the ride home from school. In art, we rarely study the glint of sunlight on the petals of rain-moistened sunflowers. We study instead the twenty-four-by-thirty-six-inch four-color reproductions of van Gogh's paintings.

Community-based art education uses the creative process as a means to investigate and to express personal and collective reactions to the real, living environment. The community is the arena of engagement between the curious child and the fascinating world. The less filtered, distorted, masked, and weakly duplicated this raw material is, the less filtered, distorted, masked, and weak the subsequent artistic expression can be.

It Enhances the Transferability of Learning

Learning theory tells us that the learning acquired from one situation is transferable to another situation in direct proportion to the similarity of the two situations. Thus learning to play the violin will afford the learner more knowledge and skill in consequently playing the cello than in playing baseball. If studying the architecture of the Acropolis offers useful though oblique rewards to children's current life, it would seem that experiencing and studying the spaces, objects, and patterns of one's own community would result in a more informed and capable member of that same com-

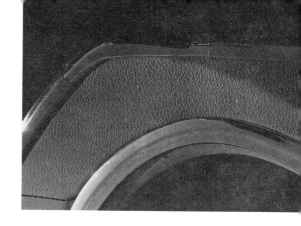

munity. Since the community is the very place and subject of the curriculum, the knowledge and skills acquired through this approach to education are the same qualities necessary for present and future active and successful membership in the community. Of course, one should be made aware of the Acropolis and the possibilities of balance, proportion, and order. This knowledge will prove of inestimable worth in critiquing and improving life as we now live it. The choice here is not between offering our children the richness of the past versus that of the present but how to use each, in what order, and to what ends.

It Nurtures Self-Identity

Achieving a clear and appropriate sense of personal identity and worth is an ultimate goal of all education. Using the community as an educational resource honors this social value in the most direct way by focusing the curriculum on children in their environment. Mapping out places and events and things in the personal life of the child, community-based curriculums then proceed to explore the widening web of life that constitutes more distant and subtle relationships.

Bringing the objects, people, and places of the child's immediate environment into direct contact with the child allows that child to form significant relationships that in turn make up a cared-for neighborhood and world. This subjective, interpretive approach to the "world out there"

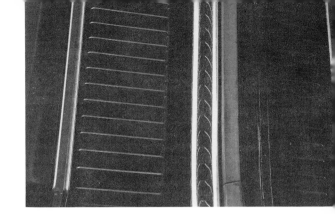

is how artists in general deal with their world: firsthand and vividly. Making art is always a reflective experience because it is always asking, What does this *mean for me?* How do *I feel* about this? Art brings together the artist and the model, the viewer and the seen, the investigator and the object of study. The indeterminate interaction between them creates the drama and the triumph of art. During this creative process, what is discovered is not only the nature of the world but, of equal importance, the nature of the self. This self-discovery is the basis of self-identity. We decry systems that impose identities and codes of behaviors on their citizens. Yet when it comes to our own system of schooling and government, we think this a good and necessary thing to do. Community-based art education is an attempt to promote self-discovery through firsthand encounters between children and their world.

It Nurtures Self-Esteem

Much has been written recently about the importance of self-esteem in the healthy development of the child. People who esteem themselves positively engage more frequently and successfully with their world than do people who have poor self-regard and who consequently experience themselves as alienated from the world and its rewards. Self-esteem is nurtured in many ways. One, certainly, is by acknowledging and affirming the legitimacy of the life one has. Before there can be positive regard

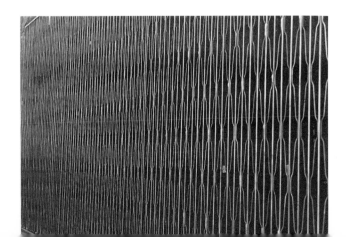

there must first be regard. A curriculum that is about something other than the lived life of the child declares in an oblique but real way that the life of the child is not worth studying. And, as Ralph Ellison points out in *Invisible Man*, people who don't enter history—that is, who do not appear in texts—are not studied. Those whose lives do not appear to warrant biographies and autobiographies are essentially invisible. The penalty of invisibility is that there is no source or repository of pride in accomplishment. Likewise, there is no source of moral reflection or social conscience.

Self-esteem first requires the presence of a *self*. A self is constructed from its myriad associations. The source of these associations, especially for young people, are the people, places, things, and events of their community. Curriculums that dismiss the community as the primary issue of study dismiss the origins and the meaning of children's lives, thus impeding the essential task of achieving positive self-esteem. Curriculums that acknowledge and make use of the association between the child and the community create a productive foundation for the cultivation of self-esteem.

It Encompasses Children at Risk

But doesn't community-based education, predicated as it is on greater student responsibility and autonomy, have in mind an ideal student and

an idealized classroom of students? How can this approach work with the actual students we so often have, those who, damaged by their home life and their times, come to school unprepared for learning? No responsible teacher would, or should, adopt a method of teaching that might jeopardize the effective conduct of his or her classes. A serious response to these questions is necessary.

Teachers who work with children at risk know that conventional curriculum content and conventional teaching strategies are often ineffective. A curriculum that is irrelevant to children's current issues is poorly received, and passive learning invokes a weak response. Educators know that parental involvement is essential if children at risk are to remain focused and productive. For children who do not succeed in the mainstream curriculum, community-based field work offers practical experiences that have immediate and conspicuous rewards. Individualized, small-group task forces provide a more effective social setting for learning than large-group settings. A network of professionals, citizen volunteers, and parents is frequently gathered to support and socialize the special learner.

The hallmarks of the best educational reforms geared to children at risk are identical to the hallmarks of community-based art education. This approach is *not* predicated on the ideal learner and classroom but is instead based on working with *all* students, even the ones who are least successful working within the present curriculum.

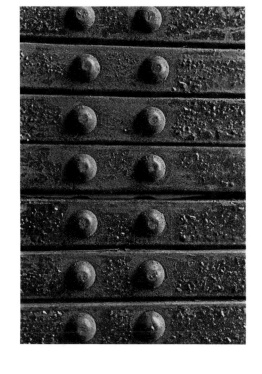

Community-based art education represents a real alternative to prevailing practices. It originates from different intentions than do the programs created for children at risk, but the remarkable similarity in strategies can be said to substantiate the reasonableness of this approach for all students.

It Reveals Hidden Dimensions of the Community

A community is not simply a conglomeration of people and places; it also involves a pattern of interaction. The qualities that animate a particular community and give it its special personality are also its invisible but very real values, laws, and ideas. Only with great difficulty can one learn about these vital characteristics of the culture by looking at slides or reading a text. Subtle things like values, fears, and prejudices are hardly ever revealed to outsiders, and the mental sets of outsiders are so strong they can mask and distort what little is offered to them. The mental landscape is best perceived by those who actively participate in it. Since it is community based in both place and subject matter, this program provides students with an opportunity to study these vital but otherwise hidden dimensions of their community. By having family and friends in the community and being residents themselves, students come to know and appreciate the qualities of their community revealed only to "family." This

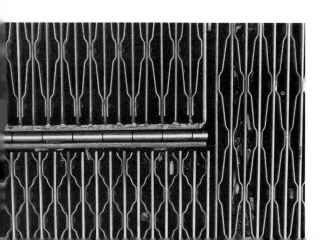

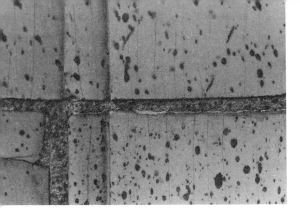

deeper understanding and these deeper feelings can't help but make the art these students produce similarly deeper and more subtle.

It Builds Community Cohesion

One of the many criticisms of contemporary society is that the socializing effects of living in an intact community are no longer available to many of our children. The disappearance of community may turn out to be one of our severest failings. But this is not a new phenomenon. Paul and Percival Goodman noted this in *Communitas*, as did Jane Jacobs in her book *The Death and Life of Great American Cities*. Lewis Mumford has pointed out the failure of contemporary cities and automated workplaces to provide a humane, congenial context for living. All social critics know that a community is more than a collection of densely packed structures and systems. Proximity alone does not create community. High-rise apartment complexes, rush-hour transportation, and megamalls clearly demonstrate this fact. A community is the sum of the rewarding interactions among people sharing common attributes. Interactions based on shared values make people care about the fate of their neighbors and make giving time, sharing personal resources, and performing acts of kindness obvious and appropriate things to do. The integrity of a community, meaning the degree of expressed care that all its members have for all the others, makes living

in that community safe, warm, and congenial.

America has suffered the unravelling of community over the last several decades, and the subsequent losses have been profound. There is no social or physical center that provides common ground for all parties. Instead, we are fracturing along special interest lines, turning away from each other, finding security and solace in smaller parochial associations. In economic terms we are experiencing the shrinking of the middle class— the historic center of American democratic dynamics—while at the same time we are seeing the expansion of the very poorest and the very richest groups. Jonathan Kozol's *Savage Inequalities* searingly describes the consequences of a nation of people giving up on "the other" and caring only for their own kind. We are divided by race, ethnicity, income, sexual preference, and religious belief. These distinctions, naturally come by in a nation as large and as complex as our own, have created exclusionary subcultures that all too often foster suspicion of (or certainly indifference to) and, at worst, hostility toward people and practices outside their domain.

One of the great divides in America is that separating the community of taxpayers from the community of the public schools they are required to support. Hard-working, overburdened teachers and administrators feel undervalued by the community. They are required to cope with damaged and needy children from dysfunctional families and at the same time are

denied the necessary resources to fulfill their mandates. The community feels overburdened by taxes for all forms of public service. And, having little contact with and input into the schools, citizens are uncertain about the cost benefits of the schools as they are. As a result of all these realities, children and their education suffer. Clearly, a major shift in perceptions, values, and consequential behaviors is necessary if we are to break this cycle of deterioration, which is leading to the collapse of one of the greatest contributions of a democracy, free universal public education.

The health of any system, and education is no exception, is the outcome of strong, positive working relationships among all parties to it. Employing the community as a primary educational resource is an unequivocal strategy that addresses the current dysfunctional relationship between schools and the communities they serve. Family, network, and systems therapies are predicated on the knowledge that dysfunctional behavior by any of the members of a family is the result of the incompatibility of *all* partners to the family system. Blame is not sought or assigned to a particular member; each member contributes to the entire family's dysfunction. Unshared and unexpressed worldviews, inadequate communication, and unexamined values all contribute to the frustration, anger, isolation, and all too often abuse and neglect of one or all family members. So too the present dysfunctional relationship among the members of the educational system. Currently, the debate focuses on which

member deserves the most blame for our failing public educational system: indifferent students, unsupportive parents, burnt-out teachers, indifferent administrators, parsimonious taxpayers.

Certainly there is enough evidence to demonstrate the dubious contributions of each. What is more important, however, and too seldom observed is that the behavior of each is the consequence of the behaviors of the others. There are indifferent students because there are irrelevant curriculums, overcrowded classes, and overburdened teachers unable to care for them adequately. There are unsupportive parents because they don't know the content of the curriculum or how to support it. Burnt-out teachers have given their time and heart and soul to their students but see their efforts to be ineffective and unacknowledged. This madness must stop. A community divided and divisive will continue to collapse if new, more productive relationships among the parties are not established. Community-based education establishes a new agenda for public education and for communities. It declares that because we are all parties to our present misfortunes, we must all be party to the establishment of a new order. This order is the exact replication of the order of our democracy: participation of all for the good of all. Although the focus of this text is art education, the basic thesis of community-based education is applicable to all subject areas and to a general understanding of the proper relationship between school and society.

It Builds Closer Relations Between School and Community

Whatever the effectiveness of the educational program, because the activities of most schooling take place almost entirely within the school building they are often invisible to the community. And just as the processes and rewards of education are invisible to the community, the activities of the community are likewise invisible to the students. This mutual isolation has a negative effect on students. And the invisibility of the positive effects of its tax dollars often breeds the suspicion in the community that this costly responsibility pays few dividends. A community-based art program avoids these pitfalls because it encourages, indeed depends on, mutual visibility and participation. Instead of open-house exhibitions of student artwork once or twice a year, this curriculum, in both its processes and its products, is constantly in communication with the community, enhancing not only the art classroom and the school, but the community itself.

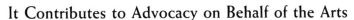

It Contributes to Advocacy on Behalf of the Arts

It is no secret that support for the arts in public education is eroding and that as a consequence the number of art specialists and art programs is declining. The reasons for this have been debated by arts and art education organizations for some time, and many remedies have been put forward, from formulating art education along the lines of the more "basic" disci-

plines, such as history, math, and literature, to passing laws legislating graduation credits in the arts.

Community-based art education proposes still another contributing factor to the eroding support for art education in public schooling—and another remedy. Prevailing efforts to ensure art education in our public schools focus either on requiring it by law or making art education resemble more acceptable intellectual disciplines. Community-based art education offers an approach to art education that retains all the creative and expressive qualities of the creative process and *inherently* builds a supportive constituency of parents, citizens, and community.

The case for the arts in public education is already lost if the effort to convince parents, administrators, and concerned (read, irate) citizens occurs at budget or legislative hearings. Claims put forth at these times about the necessity of the arts can't help but be interpreted as self-serving petitions for job retention. The position of community-based art education, its whole outlook on curriculum design and teaching methodology, is to demonstrate class by class and day by day, in the community and *with* the community, the rewards the arts bring to *everyone's* quality of life.

Community-based art education is always conscious of the community, and the community of it. Community-based art education is out in the community interviewing people, researching history, participating in

local celebrations, enhancing public places, building networks of resource consultants to the curriculum, and visualizing the heart and soul and face of the neighborhood. The art teacher employing this approach is familiar to hundreds of people of the community, has already spoken to and demonstrated the art program to many citizen associations, has already had students' work installed all over town, has the whole school glowing with the presence of art. And does so not to lobby for an art program but because this *is* the art program. This *is* its means, its material, its proper arena, and its ultimate mission: to enhance the life of all who come in contact with the arts.

3 Beginning Where We Are

Inaugurating a Community-Based Art Education Program

Every teacher draws on various aspects of the community: field trips, Show and Tell, and Parents Night are all basic features of the school year. My point is that we need to push what we now use primarily as interludes in the educational process to center stage. Shifting the community and its relation to the school from the periphery of the curriculum to the epicenter should be a gradual process, one that allows everyone involved to become comfortable in the new relationships established, accommodate the new responsibilities assumed, and reap the rewards that follow from their contributions.

The basis of this approach to education is always to start from where you are and from your strengths. No matter what is taught or how it is taught, every school system comprises the same groups of constituents— the students, their parents, the teachers, the administrators, and the community—all of whom are always present and essential.

These groups have different effects on the program and different contributions to make; each, therefore, needs to be considered in terms of its particular needs, its resources, and its impact on the program. Each group, too, influences the others, and we would do well to utilize that influence to our advantage. In every school, these groups have different constellations and characteristics: in some, there is a powerful student body; in others, power is centralized in the administration; still others boast a strong parent-teacher organization. Whatever the working relationships that currently exist in your school, it is essential to know them and use them accordingly. In this chapter I want to discuss how the groups that make up the educational community can be introduced to community-based art education. Each will be dealt with separately in order to detail its particular needs and resources and show how its members' support can be enlisted.

Teachers

Although readers of this book may come from any of the five constituencies and may in fact be members of several simultaneously, I will assume that you are most likely a teacher and begin the discussion of initiating community-based art education from this perspective.

Let's talk plainly. Our aim is to shift the use of the community from its prevailing one as an interlude, a diversion, or an enrichment to one in which it is the primary educational resource. Any change in practice, no matter how welcome and promising, produces a degree of disruption and legitimate anxiety. To initiate change with the least degree of disruption, let's begin, paradoxically, with the status quo: the best and strongest lesson we currently have, regardless of whether or not it includes any community involvement. Beginning where we are—and where we are at our proven best—will afford us a basis on which we can subsequently build.

By way of example, I offer one of the lessons I used when I was teaching art in the high schools of New York City. It was figure drawing—specifically, classical gesture drawing using expressive line to capture the essential movement of the figure. As usual, I employed student models to sit or stand in characteristic poses. I showed my students the work of Daumier and Delacroix and Degas to illustrate my points. The students were pleasant, the class fun, the drawings nice. We shifted the lights, we changed the poses, we investigated new material, we read Nicholaides and Hirschel, and we made substantial progress. After the drawings were finished we hung them up, we talked about them—about what was successful and why—and then we did them again (and again). Finally, we put up the "best," appropriately labeled, in the hall display case. Voilà: art education, of a kind.

Now let's see what happens when we transpose this unit to the context of community-based art experiences. We will start off very simply and very easily, but eventually we will see dramatic results. The class will venture outside the classroom—at first not very far—to gain a broader, deeper perspective on the issues of gesture drawing.

Our initial journey is to different areas of our own school to see where the action is. First, we simply walk around, not drawing, just looking and finding as many different places as we can where people are authentically engaged (not posed) in necessary activity: walking down the hall; going up or down the stairs; sitting or squirming through classes; roistering about in the lunch room; cooking food; cleaning the floors; fixing the windows; running, jumping, throwing, and catching in gym; combing their hair in the locker room; and so on. Coming back to class with our notes from this excursion, we discuss our findings. What a huge range of activities and gestures and positions we have encountered! (Even now, I blush at the embarrassingly constrained range of poses I provided in that earlier class in gesture drawing.) How do we attack this broad spectrum of living gesture? After heated debate about what would be best, we decide to break into groups of five to seven, each beginning with the activity most amenable to its members' own natural gestures and preferences. Next class, equipped with hard-backed pads and soft pencils, the groups set out on a half-hour excursion. Their instructions are to allow their eyes to follow the action, and their hands to follow their eyes. No composing, no refining, just capture the action and bring it back. Our destinations are the stairwell, the gym, the lunchroom, and the locker room. Half an hour (more or less) later all (more or less) return and hang up their work by group. Animated discussion ensues, and honest, strong work (for the most part) emerges.

The drawings reveal something interesting, something we didn't anticipate. Even though the figures have no features, some students can guess who is being depicted just by gesture and posture and context. We decide

59

that during our next session we will again use the gesture-drawing approach, but this time look more intently and subtly, and employ line quality more suggestively, to see if we can capture the essential personality of the individual as expressed in particular gestures, posture, and movement of head, hands, and frame.

Off we go again; this time each student is to zero in on one particular quarry. Again we return to the classroom to see what we have "caught." Now we can identify many more people. And now when we discuss the work we analyze more critically the appropriateness of the line quality each student has selected to catch a subject's personality. Out of this comes the observation, Why stick with soft pencils? Some subjects are better caught with hard lines, some with charcoal, others with pen (or brush) and ink. Again we go after our quarry, this time more appropriately armed. . . .

Can you see how the classroom is being used as the arena for discussion, reflection, and decision making, and how the community (in this case, the school community) is the research site, the raw material that is explored, discovered, and mapped? Can you also see how easy it would be to extend this premise? Suppose, for example, that students now feel more confident in their ability to capture the essential and revealing movements of people in the process of living their lives and that the subjects we have to choose from within the school grounds are beginning to appear rather tame. The students are ready to test their prowess on wilder game: let's go outside!

The school in this example is in a small town. Next to the school is the town park, where neighborhood children play and some older folks walk or sit. The town library is a few yards away, and a nursing home a bit beyond that. What begins as a way of sending the class to a strategic location soon evolves into the idea for our next project, to be entitled "Our Town": a mural of dozens of town folks going about their daily business. To be displayed first in the school cafeteria, it will then go to the town hall, gracing its walls during town meetings and local elections.

Returning from our sojourns in the school and community, we come across those first gesture drawings of student models. How stilted they now seem, how wooden, how purposeless. Nicely made perhaps, but not about much.

Students

What group could be more amenable to community-based art education than the students? It is fair to say that on any given day most students would rather be outside than inside, not merely because they can play outside and must work inside, or because they are uninterested in learning and acquiring new skills, but because schools are the way they are. Everyone reading this book knows that life outside school is different from

life inside and that most students and—dare I say so?—most teachers prefer life outside.

So let's expand the curriculum, the premises, and the pedagogy to accommodate this ubiquitous preference, not for hedonistic purposes only but for invigorated teaching and learning as well. Here again we will begin with the familiar and then extend it in the direction of other aspects of the community to see how we may invigorate instruction by joining these two domains.

We begin with self-portraits, a conventional art lesson and a topic to which everyone can relate. The unit offers instruction in such fundamentals as careful observation, tonal differentiation, proportion, simple anatomy, and texture. Because studio experiences help establish the historical context of self-portraits, the work of several well-known modern artists—Oskar Kokoschka, Käthe Kollwitz, Egon Schiele, Max Beckmann, and Alice Neel—is viewed and discussed. By studying the work of these artists, students are able to look keenly at the features of their own facial anatomy and add to this close observation a personal interpretation of how they feel about themselves. The resulting work is well seen, is competently rendered, and reveals the personality of the individual who made it. The drawings are displayed in the classroom for several days and elicit much animated commentary from fellow students. This is all in all a rather classical art education unit, but if executed competently, it helps

students develop real skill and absorb a great deal of information.

If this basic self-portrait activity is to be extended to embrace the community as an essential educational component, it may proceed in the following manner. We will base the unit on the premise that underlies this whole approach to education: that expression and commitment, even learning itself, are richest when they emanate closest to home. Therefore, this unit begins, in fact, *in* the home. The first phase of the unit asks students to find the place in their own home that feels the most secure to them. It might be their bed, a couch, a spot by a certain window, or their place at the kitchen table. They are then asked to render it in such a way as to convey to us, back in the classroom, not only what is there, but also how it *feels* to be there. When they bring their work into class, we discuss how line, color, tone, and materials, along with the contributions of the literal content, can suggest attitude and value. We also discuss the different choices people have made and on what basis they have made them.

In the next stage of the unit, students go back to those same special places, but this time they are asked to include themselves in a typical position—cuddled up, hunched over a book or a plate of food, lying on the floor playing a game, zoned out, or slumped in a comfortable recliner watching TV and munching potato chips. The work they bring into the next class is clearly more expressive, humorous, and revealing of who they

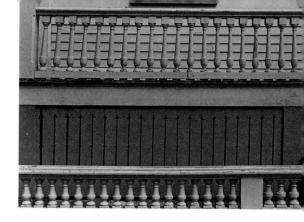

are as a personality, not simply as an array of inherited facial features.

The next phase is more adventurous still. Instead of an individual self-portrait, we will all do a portrait of just one person. We will all go to that person's residence and follow her for a week as she goes about her usual activities. We will draw and paint our interpretations of her house, the route she takes to school, and the neighborhood places she frequents. A student who lives near the school volunteers to be the portrait subject. The first day (having of course received permission from the student's parents and all pertinent others), we pack up our equipment and follow the student on her five-minute walk to her house, an apartment in a six-family building. We meet her mother and her younger siblings, and although it is quite crowded, we are shown around by our classmate and her rather dazed family. No drawing is done during this session; instead, we use the time to get acquainted and to map out the logistics of our subsequent visits. We say our heartfelt thank-yous and good-byes and leave a houseplant as a small token of our appreciation. The next two visits produce a number of sketches and quick studies, which are brought into class for further development in subsequent sessions.

While this more considered work is going on, the class becomes interested in the family history of the student whose portrait we are creating. At our request she brings some family photo albums to class and describes her family's history as far as she knows it. Although her parents

were born in America, one set of grandparents was part Irish and part Indian and the other set was from Portugal and the Cape Verde islands. The family albums and the related stories prompt a number of students to create collages using sketches and magazine images illustrative of the family. Other students decide to make an illustrated book recounting some of the family stories.

When everyone's work has been completed, we display the results in the art room and invite the student's entire family to the opening reception. They are hesitant to accept at first, but a special invitation made and signed by everyone in the class coaxes them into attending. To reciprocate, the family insists on bringing to our little vernissage an array of home-baked goods typical of the cuisines that are part of their heritage. Also invited are the favorite teachers of the student whose "portrait" is being exhibited, as well as the school principal.

Here, the creative process has served a relevant purpose for the students—and for parents, teachers, and administrators—in terms of their individual values. And the enterprise has brought all these heretofore separate groups together, revealing their common values, needs, and interests. Not only did we all have a good time, but it was an important moment in school-community relations that established the grounds for a mutually advantageous working relationship. The real life of these students became both the essential subject of study and the focus of the art

program. Line, color, form, and texture were the vehicles, the *means* of instruction, not the goals of instruction as is so often the case in the subject-centered curriculums we now have.

Parents

The community members with the keenest interest in the quality of education provided by the schools are the parents of the children who attend those schools. Whatever their relationship with their children's schools, parents, more than any other constituency within the community, are open to greater involvement.

It is common knowledge among educators that informed parental support is a major if not the single most important predictor of a child's academic success (Haynes; Weitlock). Yet educators also know that all too frequently parents are unable to provide such a supportive social context. Nonetheless, any degree of parental participation will enhance the effectiveness of this program.

Like everyone else, parents have full schedules working and raising a family. They have little time or enthusiasm for any further commitment of their resources, even when it involves their children's education. In addition, parents are tired of being promised much by one educational innovation after another only to have their children receive ambiguous benefits. Like the rest of us, what parents want to see are relevant and

conspicuous results. Only then will they support their children's education with their time and money. Therefore, we need to acquaint parents with this program through demonstrated results.

Suppose we do the following: We invite the parents of all the children in the class that has just completed the portrait of one of its members—which has in fact become a family portrait—to the exhibit. Students make personal invitations requesting the presence of their parents or guardians at the exhibit (these can be block-printed or hand-calligraphed, and provide an additional opportunity for community-oriented activity). If their parents can't attend, the children are encouraged to invite older siblings, relatives, neighbors, or any other significant adult from the community. The principal is asked to welcome the guests and provide encouraging words about their children's efforts and the program in general.

The evening arrives and most of the invited guests attend. The exhibit is well mounted, well displayed, and well labeled, and there are light refreshments thanks to the school cafeteria and the food service workers. The principal, not unmindful of the upcoming school bond issue, greets the students and their guests. After everyone has browsed the exhibit, escorted by the children, the teacher introduces the principal and thanks her for her critical support for the program. The pleased principal reciprocates and goes on to describe the educational and aesthetic results of the art program for the children and for the school in general. One of

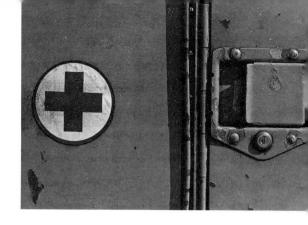

the students describes the origins of the exhibit, and then the student whose "family portrait" has been painted tells about the rewarding experience it has been for her and her family and how it has helped her make new friends and learn more about her own family. Finally, the child's mother, who admits her initial discomfort about the project, speaks of the special reward of knowing so many fine children, now such good friends of her family. Comments from the audience of parents and children are solicited and warm exchanges ensue. At this point the teacher asks if any other parents might be interested in participating in the education of their children by making their expertise, time, or resources available to the class. To help them itemize the resources they may wish to share, she distributes and briefly explains a prepared form listing the possibilities.

In my experience, most parents initially believe that they possess no particular expertise to contribute to the schools, or even if they do, that they do not have the time to share it. Both issues must be addressed immediately. In terms of possessing valuable knowledge, the teacher can easily and simply convey that whatever the family background and living conditions, the artifacts of their lives are of vital interest as desirable and valuable educational resources.

Do you live in an apartment? a private house? with relatives? in a shelter? a trailer park? a condo? Wonderful! We are interested in how we *all* live, how it looks, how it feels. Are you Lutheran? Catholic? Jewish?

Buddhist? Hindu? Muslim? Great! We are interested in your holidays, your special clothing, the special food you eat. Do you have any old family photo albums? Do you have stories of your family? Are they from Puerto Rico? China? Poland? Italy? England? Vietnam? Mexico? Fantastic! Tell us stories of the old country, introduce us to customs you still practice, to food identified with those places. Do you work? Good! Bring us there, or talk to us about it. You don't work? Even better! Tell us about that and how you spend your time. Can you get us any material for our projects, stuff from your house, your workplace, or your neighborhood? Can we come to your house? Can you show us around your neighborhood? Can you introduce us to some interesting folks you know? Are you free for only an hour this year? for an hour a month? more? less? Great. Any amount of your time is valuable. Do you have any ideas about how our class can use our own resources in the arts to work on a community-based program you know about or are involved in—projects like creating books and reading them to residents of the nearby nursing home or to children at the daycare center, projects like making posters for the Community Drug Watch Committee or for the Neighborhood Improvement Society or for the Community Center Festival Committee? Any other ideas?

By showing parents that every life, every aspect of the living community, is of inherent interest and that any amount of donated time is welcome, we encourage parents to contribute something to the program.

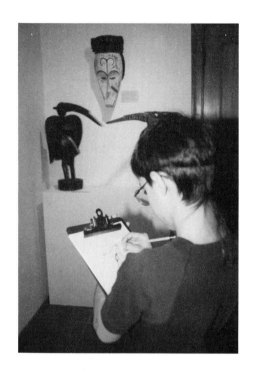

The parents (with the help of their children) fill out the forms, and we collect them, promising to keep the families in touch with the program through an illustrated monthly newsletter. The next day, the children review the previous night's experiences and, after animated exchanges, decide on their next community-based art project. Assisted by Mr. and Mrs. Ortez, Mr. Welch, Ms. Chen, and Ms. Rubenstein, they will put together an illustrated "Family Recipe Treasures" cookbook—relevant, educational, creative, community-based, and tasty.

Colleagues

This community-based approach also includes the academic community, your fellow teachers. No program can succeed without their acceptance and support. Each member of the faculty rightly believes that as an educator, he or she is doing the best possible job that conditions permit. Whenever anyone introduces innovative curricular content or strategies, fellow teachers may feel that the conditions they are used to working under have become uncertain, that the innovation may disrupt their professional effectiveness. Minimizing this concern by demonstrating that the new program will bring specific pedagogic rewards and involve minimal disruption is essential. No matter how self-evidently glorious an idea is for you, some of your colleagues are going to be all for it, some will be

indifferent to it, and still others will oppose it. Therefore, it is prudent to speak first to like-minded faculty and to develop a working relationship with your fellow teachers who are already predisposed toward community-based curriculums. This is a much wiser use of your limited time than trying to win over those whose view of what a right and proper education comprises is predicated on different assumptions.

You might introduce the idea of a community-based art program with a letter to the faculty explaining your intentions. In this way, everyone will receive the news at the same time, and distortions and unfounded concerns can be minimized. A letter as simple and as straightforward as the one below might serve, although you will no doubt want your letter to reflect your particular circumstances and be written in your own style.

Dear Colleague,

As my teaching has evolved over time, I have come to realize that my effectiveness and my students' learning are enhanced when I am able to employ the resources of our community, including students' parents, in my teaching strategies. This letter is intended to describe this idea and to ask whether you have any interest in this approach, so that we might collaborate when appropriate.

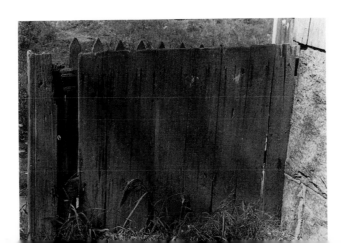

As an art teacher, I have seen that my students' work is most expressive and meaningful to them when it derives from their encounters with their real and immediate world. The world of my students is mostly bound up in the trials and adventures of growing up in a community. Because friends, family, and neighborhood events matter most, friends, family, and neighborhood have become central features of my curriculum and my teaching strategies. I call this approach community-based art education.

We use the school and the surrounding neighborhood as a resource center for materials, issues, and motivations and also for the people to help and advise us. The community around us provides a living text of our histories, our ways of coping, and even our wide-ranging possibilities. We use the art classroom as a workshop to fabricate our ideas, to discuss and analyze issues, to plan our work, and to reflect on our undertakings. The community, with its people, places, things, and events, becomes an equal component in our art program.

I am interested in meeting with other members of our teaching staff who are interested in this approach, at first to discuss the idea, then to see whether there are ways we can collaborate on certain projects or units. In my mind, our school community,

with its rich array of teachers, administrators, and staff, as well as other resources, is a vital and accessible part of a community-based approach to education. I hope you agree and are willing to discuss this further.

You might also request time during one of your inservice days or faculty meetings to make a fifteen-minute presentation outlining the program and soliciting any cooperative interest among your peers. Before the meeting it would be advantageous to speak with one or two colleagues with whom you have a strong professional and/or personal relationship and discuss the idea with them, requesting their evaluation of such a program and soliciting their support.

If given the opportunity to present a brief view of your program to the faculty, you might invite them to the Family Portrait exhibit. You might ask one or two students to speak about their participation in the project and perhaps even reenlist members of the subject family and the principal to come in and say a few words. In this way, rather than claim results that may appear self-serving, you provide actual examples as described by actual participants. You might conclude the session by asking for one or two teachers (prepared beforehand?) to describe what they are currently teaching and how they are teaching it, and then describe how

73

their efforts could be extended into a community-based program.

Your colleagues are your community of peers, and it is a good idea to inform them of your intentions before they look out the window and see you and your class scrambling around picking up bits of things and stuffing them into little plastic sandwich bags. You do not need their permission or their active cooperation, but their informed appreciation of your curriculum content and your teaching strategies will prove very helpful.

Administrators

Every teacher knows that the support of the administration is critical to the implementation of any program in the school. If by now you have an informed and able constituency in your students, their parents, and the faculty, you will already have come a long way toward achieving this support. Each administrator operates differently. Some are facilitators of the collective opinions of the students and faculty; some are more solitary in their decision making. Some are keen about curriculum reform or about evaluation or about community-school relations. Know your administrators, what motivates them, and what kinds of results they take to be meaningful. Then approach them accordingly.

If you indicate to administrators your awareness of their legitimate concerns and can demonstrate that the relevance and effectiveness of this community-based art program are at least as great as those of conventional programs, you will more successfully elicit the support of this most essential group. When the students, parents, and several supportive faculty members are effectively involved in the community-based art program, invite a key member of the administration to observe a local expedition. Discuss with that person beforehand what has preceded, and explain the purpose of this particular expedition and where you hope it will lead. Suppose you invite the administrator on a field trip with your third-grade art class, which is exploring the ground one hundred feet from the school's front door, discovering and itemizing everything they find according to color and texture. With a sketchbook and some collection bags, the children, in teams, hunt down all the blue, green, red, and brown things within that domain. Have the administrator join one of the discovery parties. After collecting their samples, the students, again in small groups, could make several collages, one for each analogous color range, around the theme "Just Outside Our Door." Again, invite the administrator to join one of these groups. In a discussion with the administrator following the lesson, you might point out the educational worth of the session: the general skills of observing, sorting, and naming; cooperative interaction; problem setting and solving; and the specific, related skills of matching analogous colors, of composition, and of collage technique (sorting, cutting, gluing, and the imaginative use of everyday materials). Provided no

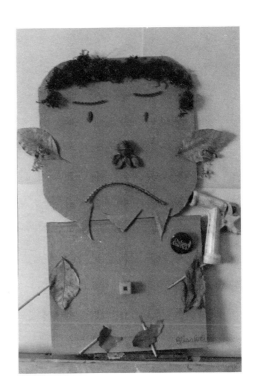

one picks up a wasp, gets stung, and has to be whisked off to the hospital, my guess is that the administrator will have a rewarding time, gain an appreciation of the educational worth of the experience, and be on your side at least sufficiently to allow the program to move forward. The next time you might invite the administrator to participate in a program such as Family Portraits, described above. If so, I am confident that you will establish the credibility of your approach to art education and, in the process, gain the necessary administrative support.

Community Members

There is a growing tide of interest within the community, especially the business community, in supporting education. More members of the community are coming to the realization that quality education should be everyone's concern, not just that of community members whose children attend school. Education is everyone's business because education affects everyone's business: private, professional, and commercial (National Alliance for Business; Phelps). Existing community-based associations have committed a significant amount of their resources to the enhancement of education in their region. Rotary clubs, business associations, chambers of commerce, municipal improvement societies, museums, and historic societies are typical community-based organizations that are committed to these efforts.

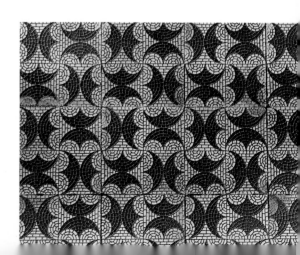

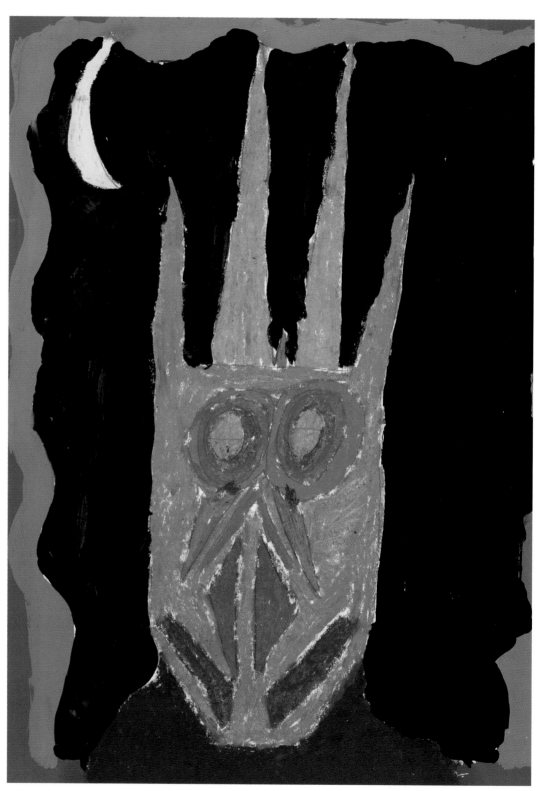

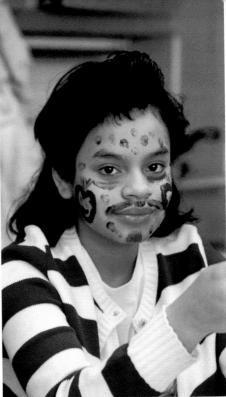

The following illustration shows how the children in a community-based arts program in a small elementary school joined with a local merchants' association to achieve a common mission. The children, in grades four to six, were used to going out on field trips, and several parents had become an essential presence in the program as volunteer teacher aides whenever the class embarked on an ambitious project. The administration had come to trust this community-oriented arts program, so when the opportunity to work in conjunction with the local merchants' association arose, the infrastructure to respond effectively was in place. It happened (and could happen again) in this way.

One of the parents whose child attended the school saw, during Open School Night, the mural the children did for the school cafeteria and was impressed by how much more pleasing to the eye it made the bleak walls of the cafeteria. The parent worked in a local store and was a member of the merchants' association, a modest organization consisting of a dozen or so merchants along a certain few commercial blocks of the town. Several unoccupied storefronts in the area had become eyesores as a result of graffiti, weather-worn posters, and the general litter of a neglected public space. It was an aesthetic insult, and it was bad for business. The merchants had discussed the matter at several of their meetings but could come to no resolution. The merchant/parent, after seeing the cafeteria mural, contacted the principal of the school about

whether the students in the art program might be interested in painting some murals on the unoccupied storefronts. The principal got in touch with the art teacher. All three—merchant, art teacher, and principal—felt this was a project that would be educationally sound, community spirited, and mutually advantageous. The merchants would supply whatever materials would be required. The principal would provide the necessary permissions and letters of support. The art teacher, along with the children, would supply the creative thinking and would execute the project.

The next phase was to bring the children (in a bus paid for by the merchants' association) to the site and ask them to help the officers of the association review the problems and the opportunities. The students loved the idea of being involved in the planning and problem-solving phase of the project. They toured the area and listened to the merchants explain the situation. Back at school they were asked to come up with some drawings illustrating their solutions. When they had done so, the officers of the merchants' association visited the school. They reviewed the solutions with the children and their teacher and offered their opinions about what they felt was appropriate. After these discussions, the children produced a set of designs agreeable to all parties. The plan called for a series of murals depicting landmark elements of the town's architecture and recommended that trees be planted and that a unified look be given to storefront signs.

The children used water-based paints and applied them on the inside of the store windows to make them weatherproof and vandal resistant. When the murals were completed, the merchants notified the local newspaper, which, mindful of its community responsibilities and its advertisers, sent a reporter and a photographer to the unveiling. Of course, the children and the art teacher were there. The superintendent found time to be there as well (a school referendum was coming up), and the principal also found an open spot in her busy schedule.

The work looked great—and so did the art program.

4 Stepping Outside: A Visual Odyssey

I listen and I forget.
I see and I remember.
I do and I understand.

AN ANCIENT PROVERB

The community contains vastly more inspiration, more surprises, and more resources than anyone can name, much less exhaust. The place is simply jumping with material to engage the minds of our children.

Teachers naturally think in terms of lessons and units and curriculums. As a teacher, I do too. This chapter describes a number of lessons or projects (I prefer to call them encounters) with which I challenged myself. The challenge was this: to take about a dozen sites next to a number of different schools in different communities and to see just *how* rich in visual resources that community might be. Both as an educator and as an artist, I wanted to see firsthand what of aesthetic and educative worth I could encounter as I walked near these schools. The brief essays about the projects and the photographs that accompany them portray what I found. It was more than even I suspected, and I hope it serves to stimulate your interest in similar adventures.

We begin with the neighborhood school—nothing exotic, nothing exceptional (other than the fact that every place is unique and crammed with resources for the taking). In all these cases, the sites were within minutes of local schools, all were public, all were free, all were safe, and all were rich with educational, aesthetic, evocative material. Another day, another season, or even another eye observing all this would have produced an entirely different range of items and experiences.

One Hundred Feet from an Elementary School in a Small Town

This journey begins by venturing no more than one hundred feet from the doorway of a public elementary school. This particular school is situated on a rather barren plot of grass, is constructed of smooth red brick, has very high windows, is in a small town of about 16,000 people, is typical for this town, and is not particularly special in terms of neighborhood, site, or anything else. Private homes surround the school on three sides, and a retirement home is on the fourth. Neither was there anything special about the day these photographs were taken. It was a mild Wednesday in September. The streets were swept clear of children, of their hoots, wails, and laughter. (They were all in school!)

As it turned out, rather than using my self-imposed limit of one hundred feet, I wandered from the front and side doors for no more than four and five seconds to take these photographs. For every photo illustrated here, I took ten more; and for every photo I took, there were ten others I could have taken.

For elementary grades, an easy project based on this initial excursion

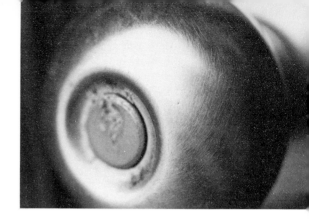

is to have the children collect material from within a one-hundred-foot radius of the school door (warning them beforehand to bypass dangerous or inappropriate material). Once they have collected, say, all the different-colored items they encounter, they can take them back to the art room and sort them according to hue, tone, and value. Then, with this material palette, they can create a mosaic mural depicting the theme "Our Town." The project can be enriched by showing the students illustrations of other people in other times engaging in a similar creative process (creating the mosaics in Rome, Constantinople, or Jerusalem, for example).

One Hundred Feet from a School in a Small City

In a rather sorry part of town, this somber school juts out of the asphalt and concrete, with no grass or trees to soften its hard profile. A twelve-feet-high cyclone fence wraps around the school, keeping what out and what in I am not sure. This school is in a city with a population of approximately 100,000. There are richer and poorer neighborhoods than this one and more and less interesting parts of town. I chose the school because it is utterly unspecial. If this area can offer some visual riches, any place can.

At first there seemed to be nothing at all here. It took a little while to grow accustomed to the landscape. Because I was looking for certain things instead of letting what was there reveal itself, I overlooked the

available material. After a while, however, the landscape came into focus, and I spotted humble but very lovely things. The first time around the school took ten minutes; the second time, an hour. Quite an interesting place, really: I never finished the third circuit. Here again I never used all of my allotted one hundred feet; fifty is more like it.

Suppose we take a sixth-grade class from this school and bring it outside, telling the children to take no more than one hundred paces in any direction from the front door. Then, equipping them with the ordinary tools of the trade—some pencils and sketching paper—we ask them to face away from the school into the community and to make as many drawings as they wish. Each student can easily make three or four such sketches of what he or she sees from a particular vantage point. Back in class they can assemble their drawings around the art classroom according to where they were situated outdoors. It will quickly become apparent that a grand diorama is in the making. With this possibility in mind, more ambitious plans for designing, then painting, a major mural to circle the entire first floor of the school could be drawn up.

One Hundred Feet from a New York City School

"Mock aesthetic" describes the building and setting of this urban school. It would have been too easy to choose an inner-city school and document the incredible cornucopia of visual outpourings stuck to and scattered

about its fringes. Everyone knows how full the inner city is with endless bits of things. Photographing the material around such a school wouldn't be convincing or provide readers with different material than they currently have. But what about schools built in planned sections of cities? These aesthetically arid zones were created to cover more space for more people for less money. The five-story apartment houses appear identical to the hospital, the supermarket, the office buildings, the motels, and the schools: the same light-tan bricks, polished aluminum rails, louvered windows, three-foot lawns, and cramped nine-foot plane trees. Open the door of one of these places and the fluorescent lights and imitation marble send memories of all the other places rippling through your system.

But even here, in this seemingly barren place, the educational potential of the community irresistibly emerges and rewards those who seek it. It may very well be that the students have a negative reaction to the neighborhood in which their school is located, appraising it as insufficiently diverse, too bland for their tastes and aspirations. This provides the opportunity for the students to take the aesthetic indifference of their community seriously, to study it, and to do something about it.

For a high school art class, a photo essay or a collection of accurate renderings of the variety of buildings surrounding the school that are visible from within the one-hundred-foot periphery becomes the theme

of their next project. These drawings and photographs are the beginning of a major sequence of art projects. While posting the drawings and photographs on the walls of the classroom, the art teacher observes that many of the buildings depicted are of very recent origin. Students begin to wonder what this same area was like years before, so their teacher asks them to search out the oldest members of the community and interview them about what they remember. The students interview their parents, grandparents, and older neighbors about where they lived and how the area looked a generation or two ago and write down and illustrate these reminiscences. They are stunned when they realize that this neighborhood, which now is all garden apartments and shopping strips, as recently as fifty years ago comprised private homes, small farms, tracts of woodland, even free-running streams. The teacher then asks whether any children have family photos that show the area as it was and brings in some early photos of his own. Drawing on the writings of Paul Goodman, Lewis Mumford, Jane Jacobs, Louis Kahn, Buckminster Fuller, and Christopher Alexander, the students eventually produce an improvement plan for their immediate community, and, as an extension of their basic idea of congenial living, a design for a utopian community, one that once again includes tree-lined streets, small parks, ponds, and other aesthetic amenities currently lost to them.

A Five-Minute Walk from a Village School

The village in question has as its commercial center a crossroad of streets characteristically named Centre Street and Main Street. In true small-town-America fashion, within a five-minute walk from the intersection, there are these venerable institutions: a luncheonette, a bank, a gift shop, a barber shop, a pharmacy, a Chinese-American restaurant, the town hall, a library, three churches, an antique-clothing store, a candy store, a dance academy, a travel agency, and a VFW hall. Two minutes more brings one within striking distance of other American life-support systems: a hardware store, a seven-day-a-week dairy and bread store, gas stations, a car dealership, a comic book and sports card exchange, an income tax preparation business, a post office, and an appliance store. The school is five blocks from all of this, a few steps from dozens of elderly people representing thousands of years of unwanted and unasked for personal history, and three minutes from architecture that goes back to the beginning of America and borrows aesthetic ideas two hundred, even three hundred years old. Running my finger along the textures within reach over three blocks, I counted 176.

A rewarding class project that makes use of this accessible and richly endowed area is to ask children to do a photo or sketch essay while at the same time chatting with people on the street or with store owners in the neighborhood about what they like most about living in the town.

They can then create an illustrated series of short stories incorporating typical village scenes. This can be made more elaborate by asking the students to investigate book design, layout, typography, handmade paper, book binding, leather tooling, gold foil printing, paper marbleizing, and so on. The resulting storybooks can be put on display in the children's section of the town library; perhaps the library board of trustees, all of whom are townspeople, will see fit to purchase some of these books for its permanent collection!

A Five-Minute Walk from a School in a Small City

Union Street: a solid name for an important street in any American town old enough to celebrate the political and social meaning of union. This city of 100,000 people has grown in response to the greater variety of tastes and needs that create a greater range of offerings than a village. Its streets offer the eye of the visual adventurer such fare as a fancy fruit and vegetable store, a Goodwill Industries outlet, a camera shop, three dry cleaners, a drive-in bank, a newsstand, a supermarket, a young ladies and gents clothing boutique, a jewelry store, several bakeries and restaurants representative of different ethnic cuisines, a department store, a furniture store, and three shoe stores. There is nothing that a normal sighted person cannot learn from a walk along Union Street about lettering, marketing, analogous color, line, tone, local and world art history, value, composi-

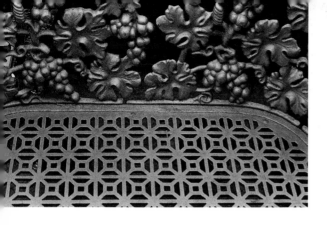

tion, expressive language, texture, contrast, fabrics, leathers, woods, metals, as well as about the issues, memories, and ambitions that animate people to do the things they do. A two-minute walk from the local school brings these riches to the students firsthand, uncensored, alive, and electric, each item and each moment an original.

America hasn't been around that long, but even in its rather brief 250-year history, it has gone through many visions of itself and expressed these visions in its architecture. Towns that have escaped the grand schemes of urban renewal retain numerous examples of earlier architectural styles and offer the community-based art program superb and accessible material to study and work with. The teacher can invite a member of the local historical society to come to class and give the students an illustrated overview of the architectural history of their area. This can be followed by a guided walking tour of the same area on which the buildings still exhibiting signs of these evolving styles are pointed out. The next excursion may be a sketching tour of the area, this time with a view toward eventually combining several works into one diorama. Returning to the classroom studio, the students can then design and execute the large painting. Eventually, the completed piece might be installed in the offices of the historical society, which could perhaps be induced to host a reception for the artists and their invited guests. At the reception, some elderly

members of the historical society could recount their memories of these bygone places, as well as the horse-drawn wagons, the gas streetlights, the itinerant vendors, the ice men, and so on. In this way history becomes real, the generations meet and converse, houses become historical texts, and art becomes authentic and vital communication. The community—its people, places, and institutions—becomes whole.

A Five-Minute Walk from a School in a Large City

At an ordinary pace, it takes about four and a half minutes to walk this block. I spent four hours here, and each time I traversed it, it had recreated itself into a new form as people, vehicles, and items constantly either moved themselves or were moved about. What an incredible display of the variety of human imagination, pouring out idea after idea, in endless virtuosity! No single mind could have the audacity or the originality to create such a cacophony of sights and sounds, art and music. What a sumptuous place a metropolis is, a coming together of people, histories, and inclinations into a mix that emboldens and tests the scope, standards, and imagination of the people. Nothing ordinary or tempered along this street: "Persian" carpets from Taiwan, Spanish glass and ironwork, Venetian chests, fancy kitchen appliances from Germany, and an entire truck-load of bogus Flemish stoves. I only walked along the street level of this

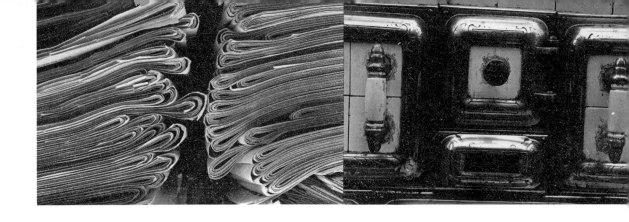

canyon. What lay inside these treasure troves—on the second, third, fourth, fifth, and sixth floors, or in basements—I have no idea. Can you just imagine?

Anything can and mostly does happen in a major city. Almost any topic studied in school can find its living example somewhere in the city, usually closer to the school than we may suspect (and this is for better and for worse). Let's take the "for better" course and see what may occur when a class studying a unit on texture and its evocative qualities uses the community as its primary resource. After exploring the idea of how important the sense of touch is in reacting to our environment, and therefore how many touch words there are in our vocabulary (smooth talker, rough character, hard day, silky voice, feeling fine, touched by your kindness, slippery person, and so on), this sixth-grade class is given what seems an impossible task. With pads of newsprint (donated by the local newspaper from unspent rolls) and carpenter pencils, the students are asked to make at least one hundred texture rubbings of different surfaces in just one half-hour excursion on only one side of the block. Go! Passersby can't help but notice dozens of little dervishes rubbing and scrubbing away, hard at work doing something uncertain.

Exhausted but triumphant, the children return to class and, for the remainder of the period, simply share their experiences of touching the varied surfaces and responding to the many incredulous questions of

onlookers. If this was done with younger children (grades K–3), chaperons would be in order and closer teacher supervision required. For younger children who are learning sorting and prioritizing skills, the wealth of rubbings could be used in any number of sorting exercises: smooth to rough, small-grained to large-grained, dark to light, linear things, spotted things, and so on. For our example with older children (grades 4–6), we use these textures to notice abstract qualities of design. From the group of texture rubbings he or she has done, each child selects one that suggests not simply the feel of the surface of the city but the feel of its dynamic energy. The students then enlarge their chosen sketch into a large-scale work, emphasizing the dynamic qualities of the feel of the city by fine-tuning the composition and employing appropriate color schemes. These powerful images, in full color and showing a dramatic contrast in textures, make for an eye-catching series when exhibited side by side in the halls of the school. The halls come alive, alive as the throb of the city itself.

A Vacant Lot

Playgrounds, school yards, parks, and streets are tamed by adult hands and imaginations. Only the vacant lot offers the anonymous hurly-burly that is at once fort, castle, bunker, desert island, jungle, and space station. It is the only piece of land that no one owns and no one is (well, hardly ever) chased from. Nothing permanent can be built here, for tomorrow

the pile of stones that served as a campfire becomes someone else's second base. The place is timeless, indefinite, and amorphous, yielding to our imagination. Every piece of rubble is fodder for our dreams. The lot in these photographs had a real treasure on it, part of an old foundation now partially covered over by piles of loose bricks. Now *this* is the stuff that dreams are made of.

An example of one of ten thousand projects that might be derived from this kind of location: Each child (in this case in grades 6 and 7) is asked to mark off a ten-by-ten-foot section of the lot. This will be his or her own domain. Any site can be selected as long as its boundaries do not overlap the boundaries of someone else's site. Then they are to take a careful inventory of what "belongs" in their special place. They can make written and illustrated lists. They can make a to-scale map of the objects (math); they can make informed conjectures about the civilization that left this debris behind (history, anthropology, social studies); they can assay the recyclable materials and their monetary worth (environmental studies, economics); and so on. They can also return to their section once each week or once each month for a school term, noticing each time what has appeared and what has disappeared (history, sociology, current events).

An alternate example: The class can decide to clean a section of the lot of dangerous and unsightly debris and in its place design and construct

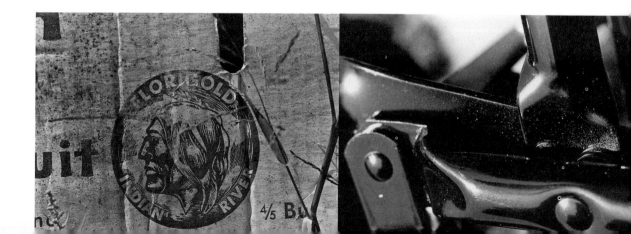

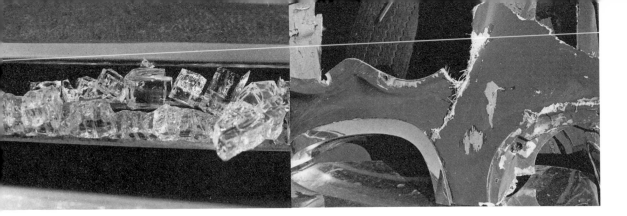

(with the help of the local civic organization or block association or local merchants) a modest playground, perhaps only some simple seating or stepping blocks or a brave planting of a tree. If this is too much, if we lack the resources to create an actual playground, at least we can cultivate children's ability to dream and hope by asking them to design a playground for this area, so that when they are old enough and do have the means to build it, it might serve as a model. And who knows, armed with these drawings, the class will perhaps march up to the local civic organization and say, Here are your children's dreams. Would you help us make them come true?

A Wrecked Car

The twisted, abandoned bodies of cars mark our urban landscape with the regularity of gas stations and fast-food restaurants. What a fall from grace! Once the family's workhorse or a young knight errant's charger, the wrecked automobile now lies broken, left to be picked and torn apart by hungry strangers mindless of the honored place it held when it was first brought home from the showroom.

Once its body stretched out in long, sinewy lines. Subtle colors of mauve, champagne, primrose, cocoa, and mint green covered its lean form. Distinctive medallions, cryptic numbers, and exotic names festooned its body. Well-appointed interiors cradled its passengers. Fierce hubcaps

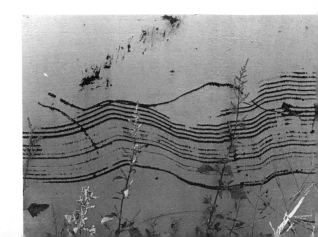

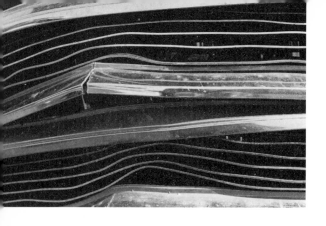

and grills told the world that its driver would stand no nonsense.

Now, its fenders pulled apart, its windows smashed in, its tires removed, its doors ripped off, and its interior slashed and soggy, the dream boat languishes. Along highways, in fields, vacant lots, and creeks, these hulks fall back into the earth by bits and pieces, a study of decay, a glut of visual extravagance. The wrecked automobile abandoned by the side of the road is too often a dramatic reminder of failed dreams and abandoned values. How to use this same object and dire metaphor for something of positive value? It is no good looking the other way; it or its surrogates will reappear. How to look at this head on and grow, rather than turn away?

This can be a particularly rewarding subject for high school students, whose lives are so fiercely wrapped up in the freedom and speed and status that only cars seem able to supply. Perhaps the first thing the class can address is simply the presence of the wreck, rendering the battered auto just the way it appears, a once beautiful now desecrated object of the American Dream. The students can draw or paint it, so that the artwork attempts to be as present and arresting and incriminating as the abandoned car itself—and, perhaps, the social ills it represents. During the time the artwork is in process, the teacher can encourage class discussions on issues related to abandonment and wreckage. Students offer personal histories, spout and challenge sweeping generalizations. Issues of personal property,

personal values, economic injustices and inequities, public and private responsibility, surface and whirl around the wrecked car. These discussions, occurring while the paintings progress, seem to deepen the visual work, transforming it from an initially illustrative piece to a more personally felt interpretation. Completing the work, the students are then asked to write a free-verse poem that incorporates the word "wrecked" in its title and the word "abandoned" somewhere among its stanzas. The final exhibition of the project might consist of an installation of the visual work, a reading of the students' poems, and a bound and illustrated copy of the poems for each member of the class.

Fences

For those people whose civilization is based on permanent sites, no more ancient construction exists than a wall or its more modern version, the fence. The photographs here are of city fences intended more for display than for protection. If a fence was only to keep people and animals in or out, then chicken wire would do. But these are sculptured things, airy relief work that sets up more a rhythmic than a physical barrier around the property. Fences are forms, expressive and descriptive displays of emotional sensibility and creative means. Unlike formal sculpture, which rarely appears in the landscape, fences are an available and common art form. A field trip of half an hour could bring dozens of different fences

to children's attention. Each one has the form, line, pattern, texture, and color of any other art form. Contemporary sculpture involves consideration of modules, systems, and professional manufacture. Fences do too.

An art project for elementary grades that derives from the presence of fences in the lives of children is as simple as this: We begin with a discussion of what the children see on the way to school each morning. At some point fences are sure to be mentioned because they are such a common element in any community. The discussion then turns to both the look and the feel of these fences. Children whose walk to school takes them by fences bring the rest of the class to these sites, noting how some are apparently meant to keep strangers out, others to keep dogs and children in. The children sketch the fences with standard equipment such as crayons and manila paper. Back in the art studio the children are then asked to depict a house and to incorporate into this depiction the one fence that sent a particular thrill through them as they passed it. Some of the fences encountered may contain a barking dog, others a happy dog; other fences may be so high that the other side remains a mystery, attracting all sorts of stories; there is the fence around the playground they could not get to, the fence of a friend's home that always seemed so special because they were escorted through it by their friend.

Not a spectacular project but one in which the children can learn about conventional art education's fascination with pattern, rhythm, and

negative and positive space and can gain an appreciation of how signs and symbols portray meaning, how investigating and drawing something can bring one closer to things and dispel disabling myths, and how the same thing (a fence this time) can have such different associations for different people.

This too about fences. I know an elderly man whose father built stone walls for farmers in upstate New York. He was paid thirty-five cents a day if the farmer supplied the stone, fifty cents if he hauled his own.

A Utility Truck

Fire fighters and police officers have been with us for a very long time. Their exploits and paraphernalia have had many years to develop a rich and exciting literature and iconography. Race car drivers, big-game hunters, pilots, and astronauts also attract the imagination and aspirations of our youth. In our increasingly electronic age, utility workers may claim a place in the pantheon of American heroes as well. We see these men and women and their gear too casually, I think. The remarkable range of their paraphernalia far exceeds the wire cutters and electrician's tape we ordinarily associate with them. Their trucks are laden with the shapes, sizes, colors, and textures of enough tools and supplies to make a hardware store look like a bicycle-patch kit—not just idle things heaped indiscriminately together but efficient and complex tools made up of many parts to get

the job done quickly and exactly. Pumps, jacks, cranes, cables, brooms, sledgehammers, cutters, pliers, winches, all are orchestrated to perform a single necessary operation: powering America.

The cornucopia of forms, colors, textures, and just plain *things* on and in a utility truck should be enough motivation to start the creative juices flowing in any group of children. The truck and its paraphernalia can most simply serve as a grand replacement for the tired still-life groupings usually hauled out year after year, the predictable Chianti bottles, broken bicycles, Indian corn, and country pottery. The utility truck is not merely picturesque, it is a live and necessary element in the real lives of the children and, of course, of the community. A visit to or by the utility truck can also be an occasion for some real-life lessons on energy use, on issues of conservation, safety, and how energy is generated and drives our technological society. A call and letter to the local utility company requesting a field trip to or a visit from a utility truck is sure to bring a positive response, especially if the truck crew is offered the opportunity to discuss topics such as safety and energy conservation.

Suppose the art teacher, along with the science teacher, arranges to have a utility truck and crew visit their middle school for a couple of hours. The science teacher works with the children on electricity, insulation, ohms, watts, amps, and so on. The art teacher works with the vehicle's welter of dramatic forms and shapes and bold colors. The elec-

trical workers could discuss color coding and the mechanical reasons for the shapes that tools come in. Then, with a perspective made more keen by showing the students the work of an artist such as Fernand Léger, whose work derived from his fascination with the power and clarity of mechanical forms, the students could set to work capturing what catches *their* eye.

Once again, the drawings, paintings, prints, relief clay sculpture, and what have you emanating from this encounter with the machine can be displayed in the art classroom or hallways of the school. But why not offer them to the utility company to exhibit in their offices, board room, reception area, or employee lunch room? This gambit may provide entrée for further field trips to the generating rooms or supply yards. While in the supply yards why not note what your class could do with some of the excess material: cable ends, wire, spikes, wood, empty drums, spools, line, and so on. How about a monumental sculpture made for and installed at the utility company? One truck, infinite possibilities.

Doorways

Every doorway is a magic portal dividing one level of reality from another, a barrier between the private dream and the public vision. Doorways tell a tale of who passes through them as well as who and what is sheltered behind them. Looking carefully at this semipermeable membrane, we can

tell the degree of privacy and anxiety that animates those within. The thickness of the wood and glass, the number and kinds of locks, bars, screens, alarms, and warning signs, all advertise their outlook on life and the degree to which they feel vulnerable in it. Like people of ancient societies, we ring the entrances to our nests with amulets, signs, and potions to ward off the evils lurking outside and to welcome loved ones.

It may be that doorways are becoming a less elaborate and conspicuous element in contemporary buildings compared with the elaborate doorways and doors of Victorian homes. So many modern doorways seem more like holes punched through walls to let a standing person through. The architectural elements that once marked off the secular from the profane are vanishing in American aesthetics: crafted doorways, fences, stairs, porches, windows, eaves, parlors, all now seem quaint. Another example of leveling the hills and filling the hollows?

In any case, once the teacher has established the idea that a doorway is not merely an entrance but a sign projecting the occupants' identity and intent, it is an easy matter to motivate a high school class to investigate the look and meanings of their neighborhood doorways. Perhaps the unit begins with a walking tour of the neighborhood (or of a neighborhood where there are many examples of different doorways), initially just observing and commenting on the doorways and entryways. Here are some questions students could be asked to address: If you were a stranger to

the area and didn't read English, what doorways would you enter? Which ones would you avoid? Which tell the most about what one might expect inside? Which keep secrets of their occupants' identity and intentions? What are the differences between residential and commercial doorways? Returning to class the next day, the class members decide they would like to return to the section of the community comprising primarily commercial buildings and do a study on the most and least inviting doorways and what architectural and design elements make them appear the way they do. Eight teams of two or three students each select a different doorway, draw it, and while doing so note who goes in and out: their dress, their gait, what they are carrying, and the expression on their face as they enter and exit. Perhaps the students inquire about the reactions the people have to the doorway and its appeal.

Gathering all these drawings and notes, the class decides to invite a local architect (or city planner or commercial designer) to view the students' work and talk about what makes an entryway appealing and what is off-putting. Issues of scale, lighting, visibility, accessibility, color scheme, and identification are all discussed. Subsequently, the class decides to use this information to redesign the doorway to the art room. With the permission of the principal and chief custodian, the doorway into the art room and the wall area around the doorway are redesigned with broad bands of color that incorporate the motto "It's all art to us."

103

Several other teachers, noticing the handsome addition to the school this entryway makes, request sketches of how the doorways to their rooms could be transformed. Many of these embellished doorways are eventually executed, creating a new and invigorated look and mood in the school.

Lettering

When I went to junior high school forty years ago, our first art lesson was to letter our art portfolios in stick letters sans serif. When I began to teach in high school thirty years ago, my colleagues' first lesson was to have the students letter their portfolios in stick letters sans serif with autobiographic illustrations. Supervising student teachers now, I visit schools where the first art lesson often is to letter portfolios in stick letters (now with serifs) with autobiographic illustrations. Aware of the immense discontinuities that have rocked our world over these last several decades—nations created and dissolved, wars begun and ended, the balance of power tipped this way and that, ecosystems crumbling, species disappearing—it is perhaps laudatory that at least one institution has remained constant in its tenets and practices: the public school lettering lesson. Somewhere in hundreds of millions of American homes lies an art portfolio inscribed with an identifying name in the upper righthand corner, with or without a picture of a favorite hobby in the upper left.

How to hybridize these practices? Step outside! Walk down any commercial street and take careful note of the variety of the typefaces, the materials, and the expressive layouts of letter forms and borders. The signature of free enterprise is to be found in part in the richness and diversity of its advertisements for itself, as expressed in its lettering.

To make the students in a middle school more aware of the expressive content of letter forms, we can ask them to find and copy several signs in their neighborhood in which the form of the letters complements what the words say. When they bring in their sketches and drawings, we can discuss how different weights, sizes, colors, shapes, spaces, and kinds of exaggeration make for expressive typography. As a test of their newly developed sensitivities in this area, they can be challenged to design a poster announcing a forthcoming event in the school for people who can and cannot read, all in letter forms. After they have met this test of their imaginative skills, the students may decide to design a book for young children who are just on the verge of reading, one they might have liked at that same age. They take favorites such as *The Poky Little Puppy, Peter Rabbit, The Little Red Caboose,* and redesign the lettering and the illustrations so that a beginning reader can "read" the adventures of a mischievous puppy, an inquisitive rabbit, or a sensitive railroad car without their parents' help. They then take these "readers" to several kindergarten classes

and test them out, making careful note of the children's critical responses and redesigning the books accordingly until a majority of the kindergartners can understand and enjoy them. The result of this project: art and effort that matter.

The Seashore

A nice thing about the seashore is that no matter how many times you visit it and give it careful attention, you never know it so completely that it can't surprise you with wonders and patterns you've never seen before. Every change of tide delivers a new collection of things to your fingertips: debris from a storm in the Azores, refuse from a ship out of Chile, flotsam from a town a thousand miles inland, all show up gratuitously along the shore. Of course, not every school is within a five-minute walk of a seashore, but I bet many more classrooms are within an accessible radius of some body of water than whose occupants actually visit it.

What a resource for art materials: driftwood, beach glass, boat parts, reeds, ropes, bottles, twine, feathers, and the bones and shells of dozens of varieties of marine life. What a fine place to study varieties of texture—small grains of sand; the protruding ledges of the earth's rock mantle; glassy shells; crusty driftwood; splayed rope; rusted spikes; gelatinlike jellyfish. Introducing a unit on gesture drawing or contour line? Watch the line left on the sand by each receding wave. Studying color? Bring a

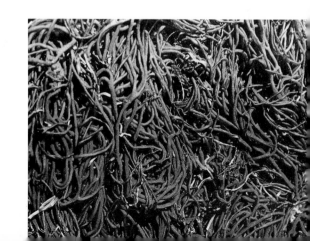

small magnifying glass with you and look at the grains of sand, crab shells, seaweed, and rusted metal.

Study the seashore carefully, record all it has to offer in one day. Come again tomorrow for a whole new lesson.

A Dock

Practically all human habitations are built near water. Most cities are built adjacent to navigable bodies of water. One of the most interesting features of a community is what happens at the point where the land ends and the water takes over. Whether the water be river, stream, bay, ocean, lake, or pond, docks are where waterborne items are processed for land-based consumption and land-based products are set upon or into the water. There is something grand about the size and heft of things on the docks. You sense that the scale of the people, things, and tasks are larger on the docks than they are inland. And some of the most gentle shades of blues, tans, greens, and grays are found there. Whole new vocabularies of texture, tone, and hue—and everything moving: water, boats, lines, birds, and people in a slow and heroic rhythm quite unlike that of the land.

Unfortunately, the water's edge has been cut off from the population of most American communities. Now highways, commercial zones, railroads, and high fences keep Americans away from their link with water. The substance that gave them life, brought them there in the first place,

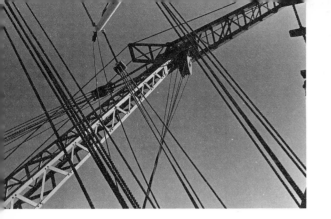

and sustains them even now is often out of reach. What a pity. What a loss of an essential aspect of our historic and aesthetic legacy. Nonetheless, more and more communities are realizing what an invaluable resource the waterside is for commerce and recreation and are providing more access. Major cities, recognizing the rewards of public access to their waterfronts, have provided it, to booming economic and recreational gain. San Francisco, St. Paul, Boston, New York, Memphis, Chicago, New Orleans, Montreal, Portland, all come quickly to mind. The resourceful teacher will find ways to return students to the water's edge.

Suppose you do get a class to the docks. What do you do now? Well, besides giving the usual and necessary warnings about wandering off, getting too near the edge, and picking up questionable stuff, why not just let the children go off in small, supervised groups and capture in drawings what they find intriguing. Sketch the most exotic things, the longest, most bizarre, most intricate, most fascinating things: the heaps of nets, chains, anchors, gears, tackle, drums. Back in class the next day, children can hang these drawings around the room and exchange stories of the previous day's adventures.

Perhaps in the discussion it becomes apparent that not many of the children have ever been to the water's edge in their own town or city before. Feeling unjustly denied this access, the students decide to do something about it by bringing their concern to the attention of the

authorities. They decide to make a scale model of a proposed waterside park and playground for their community and present it to the city council (or other local government body). Their project is on the agenda of the city council the following month, and the children, accompanied by the art teacher and several interested parents, present the model, a group of alternative designs, and a petition to create a waterside park for the community. It is signed by most of the students and teachers at their school. The reception by the local officials is cordial and peppered with stock political phrasing and vague promises. The students, and their parents and teachers, gain, in addition to art instruction about the elements of design, three-dimensional construction, and landscape architecture, a lesson in American democracy and American politics. And they will be wiser for it next time. Because there *will* be a next time.

5 Evolving Naturally

Authentic Experiences for a Community-Based Art Education Program

The first natural adventure of human experience begins with the child's discovery of the self. Tongue against gums, fingers into mouth, cheek against warmth, the infant explores its own sensations and resources. Not yet interested in the exploits of Charles the Bald or Harold the Bold or the exports of Iran, the infant reacts only to things impinging directly upon its physical self. The only curriculum of the infant besides the survival of the self is the study of the self.

Research in human development indicates that physical, intellectual, and social development occur in an intricate sequence of events, one phase necessarily proceeding from and intertwined with its predecessor. Life is dialogue. Just as the biological self does not skip any steps without serious consequences, so also the intellectual self and social self cannot skip any steps if they are to grow in like manner. Curiosity and knowledge about the self precedes curiosity and knowledge about the world. In an ever-increasing radius of curiosity, the child studies the nature of its expanding world (Clarke-Stewart and Koch; Harris).

The scope and sequence of community-based art education evolves along principles similar to those of human growth and development. It begins with the single, self-interested individual and gradually progresses to wider domains. The order of the art experiences follows this same natural progression: the classroom, the school, the family/house, the

community. We have stopped at this radius, but this spiraling curriculum may go on to include the state, the nation, the planet, the galaxy, and the universe. Starting out more modestly, we will begin our art curriculum with a series of firsthand encounters as simple as opening the door to the classroom and stepping out into the hall. What follows is a series of authentic art experiences in which children encounter the real world of their community. As in all the examples offered throughout this book, they are to be understood as the possible outcomes of particular children encountering specific locales in certain times and circumstances. They are not intended as surefire lessons, nor should they be imposed on children. Evocative as they may be, they lose their worth unless they are the natural outcomes of meeting and reacting to one's own particular life and its endlessly fascinating and uncertain ways.

School and Classroom

1. Tape the edges of a piece of paper firmly to the floor in the halls of the school. After a change of classes, pick up the paper and note the variety of shoe marks on it. Try to identify different kinds of people by their shoe marks and how they walked.

2. Do the same thing in special areas of the school: in stairways, in the gymnasium, in the lunchroom, in front of the principal's office, in an

art room or a math room, on the front steps at 8:30 A.M. and at 3:00 P.M. With these samples of the footprints of fellow students treading familiar pathways you can undertake any number of creative experiences—blowing up the footprints to mural-size paintings in invented color schemes, for example, or using them as a basis for wrapping-paper, fabric, or book-endpaper designs.

3. Locate areas of the school that have indifferent aesthetics, especially those that are just plain ugly: a dark and dingy hallway, a battered door just waiting for some handsome graphics and bright colors. Bring these to the attention of the administration with alternative designs that are more aesthetically rewarding.

4. Identify the public spaces in your school that are the most attractive and those that are the least pleasing. Document these areas by making drawings or taking photographs, and then publish the results in the school newspaper with side-by-side examples of more aesthetically pleasing alternatives. Ask for additional student and faculty input. Work with the administration and custodians to see these plans become reality.

5. Plant some flower or vegetable seeds next to the school (in window boxes or other containers if there is no soil nearby). Visit them periodically and record their evolution in a visual journal of drawings

and photographs. Label them (get the science teachers and their classes to help).

6. Create a handsomely designed and illustratively labeled school garden. Tend it as you would craft a painting.

7. Adopt a pet (fish, turtle, mouse, or lizard) and, in a visual journal, periodically record its growth and changes. Display your journal in the library along with illustrations completed in your art classes.

8. Stand in a hallway or stairway and do five-second gesture drawings of people passing by. Later develop some of them into more substantial drawings or paintings. Exhibit them in the hallway or on the stairway where the initial gesture drawings were done.

9. Notice the quality of light in various areas throughout the school and what it does to people as they go into and come out of those areas. Make sketches of what you observe; back in the art classroom develop these into paintings, drawings, or prints, focusing on how tone and value indicate form as well as mood. Get the administrative staff and the custodians to hang these artworks in their offices.

10. Explore parts of the school you don't often see: the boiler room, storage rooms, the basement, the attic, the custodians' quarters. Note how their aesthetics are distinct from those of the classrooms and offices. Draw and paint some of these off-limits areas. Discuss their

differences and similarities, and perhaps why one environment is cared for differently than another. Have a picture-identification contest in the school newspaper using these drawings.

11. Videotape or photograph a time sequence at a busy intersection in the school: a doorway, the stairs, the lockers, or the cafeteria. Notice the different sets of movements and postures in each locale. Again, use this raw material to develop paintings or sculpture back in the art room. This is also evocative material for a mural that could be mounted later in these same spaces. The themes of the mural could be issues of current interest to the students: dating, race relations, gender relations, or just what's happening.

12. Go on a "blind walk" of the school with a sighted partner. Try to establish where you are by touch, sound, and sense of space. After a while, exchange roles with your partner. After each partner has both led and been led, make images of the experience and write about them.

13. Use your school newspaper both as an art form and as a forum for your artistic concerns: submit material to each issue about an aesthetic dimension of the school. Ask for a column on this subject to be a standard feature of the newspaper.

Home and Family

14. Sit down across the street from your home and draw the building as carefully as possible. Do this at different times of day, in different weather conditions, and using different media. See how the same object takes on wholly new qualities in different contexts of light and weather. Exhibit these drawings as a group alongside one of Monet's light-study series (the Rouen Cathedral, waterlily, or haystack series, for example).

15. Draw or paint the images you see in looking out each of the windows of your home. Again, do this at different times and using a medium appropriate to that particular image and expression. Exhibit these alongside the work of the impressionist Pierre Bonnard or the work of David Hockney, and discuss the different and similar scenes and sensibilities.

16. Draw a detailed picture of your room or a space that is specially yours. Look at your picture in relation to the work of artists who also depicted their immediate surroundings, such as van Gogh, Bonnard, Wayne Thibaud, and Janet Fish.

17. Draw or paint a careful study of each member of your family. Bring in the work of the early Picasso, Lovis Corinth, and Paul Cézanne to

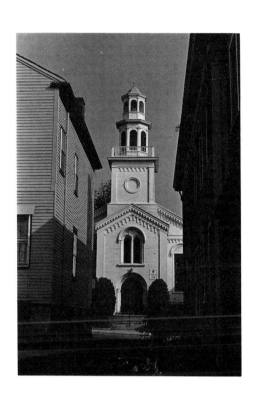

see similar circumstances and differing points of view. Next time allow yourself to be more expressive of your *relationship* with the sitter and not concerned only with portraying their physical likeness. View these later studies in connection with the later portraits of Picasso and the work of Otto Dix, Oskar Kokoschka, or Frida Kahlo.

18. Select the one item in your home that you find most precious and draw or paint it. (The work of Georgio Morandi is a wonderful comparison here.)

19. Choose someone in your family with whom you are currently having "trouble" or of whom you are especially proud and draw or paint that person.

20. Assign a characteristic color chord to each member of your family and, using only these colors, compose a "portrait" of your family.

21. Do the same thing with another element of art, such as line, form, texture, or shape.

22. Ask each member of your family to do a portrait of you in a medium of his or her choice. Compare these with your own self-portrait. Discuss the apparent and felt differences in these portraits with your family. Display these portraits prominently in your home, and invite the reactions of friends and other family members.

23. Describe (in a painting, sketch, poem, etc.) favorite places that your

family likes to visit: parks, relatives' homes, the beach, a favorite restaurant.

24. Describe your family at dinner time or at breakfast time, in any media appropriate to the setting and the feeling. (See the works of Bonnard, Dégas, Vermeer, Alice Neal, or Audrey Flack as a prompt for this.)

25. Draw your closet or one of your drawers. Don't fix it up, just do it as is.

26. Make a still life of a collection of your personal treasures. Place them on a surface where they probably are anyway, on top of the stereo or the bureau, or heaped beside your bed or in a closet corner. (Janet Fish and Faith Ringgold are stimulating comparisons here.)

27. Over a period of time, a month perhaps, collect and create a package, the form and content of which is a "portrait" of your family at home. The package could include drawings, paintings, collages, casts, prints, tape recordings of conversations, photographs, home movies, labeled charts of individual statistics. Create an environmental design piece of these memorabilia of your family for the class. Spend a day just telling family stories based on these "family portraits." (The work of Joseph Cornell is instructive here.)

28. Videotape a day in the life of your mother, father, sister, or brother, at home or at work; never get more than ten feet away from your

subject all day. Shoot what he or she sees. Screen it and videotape your subject's reactions. Play this videotape back. With your subject's permission, screen the videotapes for the class. Invite parents to an Open Movie Night. (The photographs that Minor White, Ben Shahn, and Dorothea Lange took for The Works Project Administration offer comparable work here.)

29. Tape a piece of paper on the floor of the entrance to your house or apartment and leave it there for a day. Can you identify who came in and out by looking at their footprints?

30. Draw a realistic picture of your family's automobile; then soup it up to your heart's content and the extent of your imagination, even if that is not matched by your pocketbook.

31. Ask your parents to tell you the story of how your family came to America. Write down and illustrate that story.

32. In school, put together a book containing similar stories brought in by your classmates. Give each author a copy signed by all the other authors: a class portrait.

33. List all the art books in your house. Compile a class inventory of art sources. Ask the librarian to help you catalogue and arrange them for easy access. Keep the file in your art class for reference and *use* it.

34. List all the artwork in your home: paintings, calendars, vases, bowls,

furniture, rugs, lamps, etc. Draw or paint or sculpt them, then compare and discuss them with classmates both from a personal vantage point and from a more objective position as if you were a cultural anthropologist examining artifacts of a "lost" people.

Neighborhood and Community

35. Research the holidays and festivals observed in your community, such as Flag Day, seasonal holidays, and national and local commemorative events. Design and construct flags, banners, floats, costumes, rituals, to celebrate these community events. Get involved in these ongoing festivals. Donate the flags, open a booth, design and build a float, sew the costumes and wear them. Add to your community's celebrations. (The work of Corita Kent and Jan Steward as described and illustrated in their book *Learning by Heart* offers many inspiring examples of these ideas.)

36. Identify children in the community who are shut-ins or who are in children's hospitals, orphanages, and clinics. Visit these places, survey the children's needs and abilities, then design and build toys and games for them. Visit these places again with the toys and games in hand, play with the kids, and leave the toys and games when you go. Learn about philanthropy and charity and thanksgiving firsthand. (This can be the theme of an entire year's art program.)

37. Illustrate (realistically, expressively, or imaginatively) the following things found within your community:
   - Architecture of note (the oldest, the most intricate, the jazziest, the most sedate, the friendliest, the most foreboding, the craziest, the blandest).
   - Varieties of people's faces, from youngest to oldest.
   - Rooftops, skylines, treetops, clouds.
   - Varieties of trees, flowers, shrubs, rocks.
   - Cars, trucks, other vehicles.
   - Doorways, fences, steps, windows.
   - Letter forms on business offices and storefronts.
   - Window displays.
   - Fast-food restaurants.
   - What people do to earn their living.
   - Parks and how people use them.
   - What people do for recreation.
   - Dogs; cats; birds; creepy, crawly things.
   - What men do, what women do, what children do, what the elderly do.

38. Make copies of your illustrations using print forms or another stencil process, or photocopy them, and give them to special friends.

39. Develop an exhibition around the theme "My Town on My Mind." Bring together sights, sounds, maps, and people in a comprehensive exhibit. Have guest speakers and local performers; invite the community to help sing a song of themselves. This could be an end-of-year bash in collaboration with the town government or the historical society. (See the works of Barbara Kruger for evocative examples of this perspective.)

40. Make a series of clues leading to different treasures or places of special importance to you. The clues could be visual, tactile, auditory, or oral. Have the class try to follow these clues to the "treasure."

41. Make a large map of the neighborhood. On acetate overlays, locate
    • Places of particular visual interest.
    • Classmates' homes, friends' homes, clubhouses.
    • Special places, scary places, quiet places, dangerous places, nice places.
    • Play areas, trees, vacant lots, alleys, benches, stoops, gardens.
    • Homes (or former homes) of people of contemporary or historical importance.

42. Make an illustrated map or even a three-dimensional town plan of where in the community your family goes to play, to work, to shop, and to talk. Compare your map with those of other students and

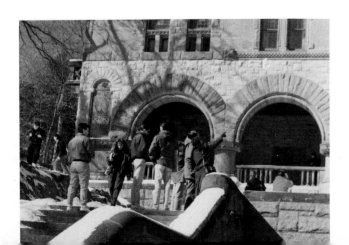

discuss differences and similarities. Bring the civics, history, and social studies teachers in on this and see what they can add to the discussions and research.

43. Locate areas of visual neglect and carelessness in your community. Record them and bring them to the attention of the authorities and the news media. Design alternatives and make sure something is done even if you have to do it yourself.

44. Trace the history of your community using only existing local architecture. Photograph and draw the houses, interview older community residents, look up related history in the library, historical society, or town hall. Exhibit the resulting work in the historical society or town hall. (See the photographs of Stephen Shore and Garry Winograd for ways of "capturing" these kinds of images.)

45. Trace the sources of local architectural designs back to their country and time of origin. Create an illustrated history of the origins of your local architecture.

46. Build a scale model of your home or apartment building and its immediate surroundings. Exhibit the model in school or in the town hall.

47. Visit places in the community that few people ever get to see, such as basements, attics, engine rooms, storage rooms, roofs, and garages; record their actual look and their felt look.

48. Locate and describe the quality of light in various places in the community. Notice how going from one light space to another affects you.

49. Do a video or photo essay of a day in the life of a local work crew, postal worker, cat or dog, storekeeper, sanitation worker, childcare worker, and so on. Invite your subjects and their friends and family to the exhibit's opening. (The photographs of Walker Evans and Margaret Bourke White can be helpful here.)

50. Videotape, photograph, or draw a single active and important locale in the community—for example, a school doorway, a bus stop, a storefront, the police or fire department, a crosswalk, or a park bench.

51. Select a ten-foot square of ground in the community—a street corner, playground, vacant lot, woodland, garden, shore line. Return to it periodically—hourly, daily, weekly, monthly—and make a photographed or drawn record of it each time. Date each record. Post your records in class periodically and discuss the changes and what that may mean for the evolving life of the community.

52. Look at and draw the varieties of front doors, windows, steps, and roofs in your neighborhood. Collect your drawings into a book about the community. Have the historical society or improvement association exhibit your work.

53. Take a given community element—the streetlights, a storefront, a

park, a parking lot—and design a practical version with better aesthetic qualities. Submit the designs to city councillors, selectmen, or the civic association for consideration in town planning. Learn about town government, town values, politicians, advocacy, design—and patience.

54. Plant flower seeds along highways, streets, vacant lots. Visit them periodically, tend them, and canvass the reactions of passersby. Document your adventures and the impact your efforts have on your fellow citizens.

55. Exhibit works of community-based art in community agencies and public places. Arrange for exhibitions in ethnic clubs, soup kitchens, public buildings, social agencies, hospitals, homeless shelters, clinics, other schools, businesses.

56. Whatever grade you are in, you have some expertise. Offer demonstrations and workshops that draw on your skills to such community organizations as children's wards in hospitals, local service organizations, and nursing homes.

57. Locate large public walls that if painted with murals could improve the aesthetic quality of the area. (The works of the great Mexican muralists Siquerros, Orozco, and Rivera provide a vast range of possibilities here.) Sketch the given site, make some preparatory designs,

identify the owners of or the parties responsible for the site, lobby for the contribution to the community the murals would provide, and appeal for funding for the cost of materials; then, when everything is in place, execute the design. (A term's project, and worth it.)

58. Design a children's park. Search the community for where children play, empty spaces, free and inexpensive materials, interested people (parents, other children, service clubs). Draw the existing site; design several alternative plans for the park and construct a scale model of one or two; give a public presentation to local officials. Construct or help construct the park when approval is received. (Work closely with your school's parents organization on this.)

59. Do the same for a toddler's playground, a park for older community members, a resting place for shoppers, a shelter for people waiting for public transportation.

60. Search out and record the varieties of lettering you find on packaging, vehicles, stores, public buildings, postal boxes, streetlights, traffic signs. Compare their styles for effectiveness of purpose, information, durability, clarity, inventiveness, impact. Keep a notebook on type-faces. Design your own typeface (for your own type of face). Using your own letter forms, write poems and messages and design posters.

61. Locate the most pleasing visual entities in your community: houses,

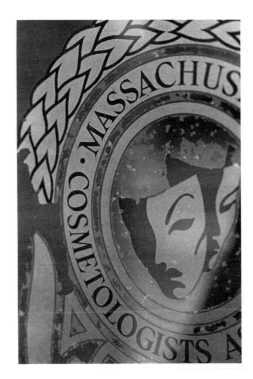

gardens, storefronts, etc. Design awards and hold a ceremony to present the citations to those responsible for designing and building these entities. Make sure the press attends.

62. Do the same thing for people responsible for insults to the aesthetic qualities of the community.

63. Witness and record previously unexperienced times of day: early morning (its sounds, light quality, colors, people); late night (its stars, shadows, altered forms, sounds); just after rainstorms. Paint, draw, or write poems about these times and circumstances. Select a time, place, and weather condition that is "just right" for you. Create artwork expressive of that "rightness." Exhibit all of these in class and discuss comparisons. (Read the haiku of Bashō and Hokusai for "just so" examples.)

64. Locate a space in the community that is special for you: a particular tree, a storefront, a vacant lot, a playground, a neighbor's back yard. Record its look, its feel. Bring a friend to it and share it. Paint, draw, or write a poem about it.

65. Take a walk with the oldest resident of the area. Let him or her guide you through the town. Ask this person to tell you about the personally observed history of each area and building. Write down the stories, illustrate them, gather them into a book, and give your guide a copy.

66. Try to match the mood of different locations in the community with pieces of music. (Listen to works by Gershwin, Copeland, Ellington, and Cage.) What does this matching indicate about the locale? Design an improved look for the area using the music as inspiration.

67. After mapping out and recording the community as it currently is, with its aesthetic high and low points, work out a plan for an improved community. Reconsider and redesign:
   • Dwelling places.
   • Commercial establishments.
   • Parks and other peaceful areas.
   • Performance spaces.
   • Government places.
   • Learning places.
   • The networks of communication and transportation.

68. Make a scale model of your designs using photos and videotapes of the present community and your preliminary studies.

69. Exhibit all this in a public space and invite the community, the town council, the mayor, other politicians, the school board, the tenants' association. Become a concerned citizen!

70. Select a block in the community that has some quality of interest or concern for you. With the other children in your class create a mural

depicting the block and exhibit it along the school's hallway. Offer to exhibit it in the town hall or the business association.

71. Each kind of weather creates a special context of light, temperature, and wind, which transforms all objects and events accordingly. Select a given neighborhood location and paint it in different weather conditions: hot and dry, rainy, snowy, etc. Once again, exhibit these works alongside works by the impressionists, who also were fascinated by weather and light phenomena.

72. Draw or paint some skyscapes, including only the barest fringes of the landscape as a reference. (Enrich this activity by showing works by Turner and O'Keeffe.)

73. Draw, paint, or write a poem about the surfaces of streets, cars, or sidewalks during and immediately after a rain.

74. Use snow as clay.

75. Divert a stream of rainwater running down a gutter. Make dams, bridges, oxbows, gorges, waterfalls. Design watercraft that can navigate these waterways. Videotape these boats coming down the stream. (Make your own Spielberg high-adventure film!)

76. Listen to the sounds objects make when they are hit by rain. Tape-record these sounds and orchestrate them into a piece of music. Choreograph a dance to this music.

77. Design and make kites. Try to invent different patterns for body and tail. (Don't neglect to fly them!)

78. Identify a place in the community where you haven't been and want to go. Pair up with someone who has been there, then go and record what each of you sees.

79. Plan a group visit to a local "no-man's-land." Why don't people go there? What stories are told about this area? Illustrate these stories, à la Grimm's fairy tales.

80. Explore one of the "site myths" of your community (a "haunted" house; a field of dreams; a mysterious tree, basement, attic, alley; scary woods; a neighbor's yard) with sketchbook, camera, and note pad. Photograph the place. Draw it, paint it, make a collage. Fantasize about it. Discuss it. Exhibit your artwork and publish a book based on these stories and images. (See the photomontages of Jerry Uelsmann and Frederick Sommer for their interpretations of these ideas.)

Want more ideas? Do any or all of the above projects with a magnifying glass; while standing on your head; with one eye closed; with a long, paper tube; with binoculars; with someone else's glasses; through colored, transparent cellophane (blue, orange, green, red, etc.); while crawling close to the ground; with ear plugs; very, very slowly; with a good friend; with your mother, father, sister, or brother; with a new friend.

On First Looking into a Gorilla's Eye

I remember a TV show about a team of naturalists who were studying gorillas. They had devoted their professional lives to becoming acquainted with these magnificent animals. The program showed the naturalists on a trip they took to observe gorillas and film their living habits. After a long trek into the mountains of Africa, the naturalists finally located an extended family of gorillas and camped nearby. One day a member of the team crept closer and closer to a group of gorillas without frightening them away and without being frightened away himself. The naturalist lay in some bushes while the gorillas fed and played nearby. Then something wonderful happened. A mother gorilla who was feeding and playing with her baby casually approached, and, reaching out, gently stroked the naturalist's face, just like that. The naturalist began to smile beatifically. It was not a smile of happiness or astonishment, but a kind of sublime glowing. It was as if he had finally made it to the other side, made contact with the real world, with the "other." He had touched wildness (actually, wildness had touched him), and it was good.

The naturalist didn't get up right away. He just lay there with that goofy smile on his face. The baby gorilla crawled into his lap, and the mother gorilla continued to feed her baby and herself; from time to time she stroked the naturalist reassuringly. When the gorillas left and he did get up, he didn't look like the same naturalist, or person, who had lain down a few minutes before. *Now* he knew gorillas.

A not so very different story: Many years ago I was teaching an art

education course and we were dealing with children's visual development. I told my students this and that about what children do and when they begin doing it. I had read the literature, I had taken courses in the area, and I knew what I was talking about. Or so it seemed. Then my wife gave birth to our first child. I spent a lot of time holding our baby, looking at our baby, listening and smelling our baby, letting him rest on my belly and watching him and me rise and fall together. When I came back to my art education class, I looked at my students and said, "I don't know anything about children yet. Let's talk about something else until I do."

Coming closer to the real world, touching it directly, engages the senses, engages our entire personhood in ways and degrees that second-hand accounts can only guess at. Encounters with the real world teach us more and enable us to care more. Building points of contact with the real world ("real" meaning the world that directly touches the lives of our students, their families, friends, neighborhoods, and concerns) simultaneously builds community. And a community engaged with its schools in the education of its youth is the prerequisite for effective schools and intact communities.

This book began with an invitation to "step outside" and allow your students, your curriculum, your teaching methods, and yourself to be invigorated by firsthand encounters with this wondrous if uncertain world. It concludes with the same invitation: extend, deepen, vitalize what you teach, whom you teach, how you teach, and why you teach. Step outside.

Selected Bibliography

ALEXANDER, CHRISTOPHER, ET AL. 1977. *A Pattern Language: Towns, Building, Construction.* New York. Oxford University Press.

CLARKE-STEWART, ALISON, AND JOANNE B. KOCH. 1983. *Children: Development Through Adolescence.* New York: John Wiley.

DEWEY, JOHN, AND EVELYN DEWEY. 1962. *Schools of Tomorrow.* New York: E. P. Dutton.

ELLISON, RALPH. 1952. *Invisible Man.* New York: Random House.

FULLER, R. BUCKMINSTER. 1970. *Utopia as Oblivion: The Prospects for Humanity.* London: Allen Lane.

————. 1979. *Synergetics 2.* New York: Macmillan.

GOODMAN, PAUL. 1960. *Growing Up Absurd.* New York: Random House.

————. 1964. *Compulsory Miseducation.* New York: Random House.

GOODMAN, PAUL, AND PERCIVAL GOODMAN. 1960. *Communitas.* New York: Vintage Books.

HARRIS, JUDITH R. 1984. *The Child from Birth to Adolescence.* Englewood Cliffs, NJ: Prentice-Hall.

HAYNES, NORRIS M., ET AL. "School Climate Enhancement Through Parental Involvement." *Journal of School Psychology* 27 (Spring 1989): 87–90.

HIRSCHEL, MILTON. 1986. *Creative Figure Drawing: Art from Life, Life from Art.* Englewood Cliffs, NJ: Prentice-Hall.

HOPKINS, L. THOMAS. 1941. *Interaction.* Boston: D. C. Heath.

JACOBS, JANE. 1961. *The Death and Life of Great American Cities.* New York: Random House.

KAHN, LOUIS. 1991. *Louis Kahn: Writings, Lectures, Interviews.* Edited by Alessandra Latour. New York: Rizzoli.

KENT, CORITA, AND JAN STEWARD. 1992. *Learning by Heart.* New York: Bantam.

KOZOL, JONATHAN. 1991. *Savage Inequalities: Children in America's Schools.* New York: Crown.

LÉGER, FERNAND. 1973. *Functions of Paintings.* Translated by Alexandra Anderson. New York: Viking.

LOWENFELD, VIKTOR. 1957. *Creative and Mental Growth.* 3d ed. New York: Macmillan.

MEARNS, HUGHES. 1958. *Creative Power: The Education of Youth in the Creative Arts.* 2d ed. New York: Dover.

MUMFORD, LEWIS. 1952. *Art and Techniques.* New York: Columbia University Press.

NATIONAL ALLIANCE FOR BUSINESS. *Compact Project: Final Report.* 1991. Washington, DC: National Alliance for Business.

NICHOLAIDES, KIMON. 1941. *The Natural Way to Draw.* Boston: Houghton Mifflin.

PHELPS, ALLEN, AND PAUL THURSTON, eds. 1989. "Public-Private Sector Collaboration in Education: Implications for Research, Policy, and the Education of Professional Educators." Proceedings of the Annual Rupert N. Evans Symposium, Illinois University Department of Vocational and Technical Education, Urbana.

ROGERS, CARL. 1961. *On Becoming a Person.* Boston: Houghton Mifflin.

THORNDIKE, EDWARD LEE. [1913] 1969. *Educational Psychology.* New York: Arno Press.

WEITOCK, THERESA A. 1991. "The Development and Implementation of a Parent Outreach Program to Increase School Involvement of Fourth-Grade Parents." Ed.D. Practicum, Nova University, Fort Lauderdale, Florida.